Raising a Child on the Autism Spectrum

Raising a Child on the Autism Spectrum

Insights From Parents to Parents

Mallory Griffith, MA, CCC-SLP &
Rachel Bédard, PhD

ISBN: 0990344541
ISBN 13: 9780990344544
Library of Congress Control Number: 2017901195
TPI Press. The Practice Institute, LLC, Camp Hill, PA

Acknowledgments

We are profoundly grateful to the many people and institutions who have supported us as we wrote this book. Thank you to TPI Press for accepting both of our book proposals, simultaneously; that was a vote of confidence! Specifically, and in memory, thank you to Dr. Steve Walfish, who randomly shared a cell phone number, encouraged us in our progress, and, after two sleepless weeks, e-mailed us our contracts. Sadly, he passed away days after we submitted the first draft of our book. With gratitude, we would like to acknowledge the rest of the team who took over following Dr. Walfish's absence: Dr. Jeff Zimmerman, Dr. Pauline Wallin, and Dr. Lauren Behrman. We appreciate the support and guidance, particularly in this time of loss for TPI Press.

Thank you to Sarah Kyle at the *Coloradoan* for helping us share our project with the community, and thank you to the many people who shared the *Coloradoan* article with family and friends across the nation.

Thank you to the many authors who published before us, including Julie Clark.

Finally, a personal and heartfelt thanks to our own families and the client families who directly or indirectly contributed to the book, cheered us on, believed in us (even beyond this project), and who share in our successes. We are lucky women to have access to such outstanding support.

Contents

Step III. Your Future Journey

Introduction

Over the years, we repeatedly have been asked poignant and heart-wrenching questions about raising children on the autism spectrum. Families frequently ask about the diagnostic process (e.g., Should we have our child diagnosed? When and how should we tell our child about a diagnosis?). All the while, these families were sharing with us the fabulous stories of their unique and gifted children—stories that highlight the power of connection, pursuing passions, and the beauty of the mind of someone with autism spectrum disorder (ASD). While we briefly considered writing the book ourselves, these are not our stories to share. Ultimately, these are the stories of families living and loving on the autism spectrum.

Together, we facilitate a group for young adults, some of whom are on the spectrum. Each week our group members inform us what kind of problems they would like to solve. They walk out with a handout of ideas to support these topics. One cold January Monday, a mom half-jokingly asked us, "Are you two writing a book?" After confidently assuring her we were not, by Wednesday we were on the phone talking to Dr. Steve Walfish, who kindly offered his cell phone number ("Let's talk!") and who suggested we had not one, but two books; he then e-mailed us the paperwork to submit a proposal. Thank you to forward-thinking moms waiting in the hall for their young adults—moms who helped us find a dream!

Following the arrival of our book contracts, we decided to give up sleeping and eating, and focused all of our efforts on connecting with families to join us on the journey of writing a book. Within a short time, our writing roster was full. In an ideal world, our authors and their children would represent a perfect distribution of demographics (e.g., gender, average family income, age). In reality, there were many more narratives written about sons than daughters, and more submissions by moms than by dads. The demographics in the book are a reflection of what was submitted and by whom. It's worth noting that, according to the Centers for Disease Control and Prevention, ASD is 4.5 times more likely to occur in males than females (http://www.cdc.gov/ncbddd/autism/data.html), and that is reflected in the contributions, as well.

This book explores the process of diagnostics, best and worst days, lessons learned, and hopes for the future for individuals living on the spectrum. Each topic is brought to life by three families per chapter to illustrate the diversity of experiences of living on the spectrum. We believe these stories will resonate with you.

As you have likely experienced, you often find yourself explaining your child to others. Because you have spent your days explaining the world of autism to others, you already know that words are tricky. Words can have powerful meaning, depending on who says them, how they are said, and the perceived intention. In writing this book, we asked parents to share their authentic voices—including the words they feel most comfortable using when describing their beloved and brilliant children whose brains work differently from ours. We have edited some of their narratives and disguised the identifying characteristics of the families to protect their confidentiality.

Please consider the differences (or similarities) among these words used to describe the children: *autism, a child with autism, my child with autism, Asperger's, Aspie,* and *ASD.* See also *quirky, odd, weird, delightfully talented, unexpectedly and welcomingly funny,* and *uneven developmental profile.* We cannot know what words you use or would prefer to have presented in this book. We do know that all of these parents wrote from the heart, with the very best of intentions. Please read with an open mind, and know that not everyone uses the same words.

As we have been told (repeatedly), Asperger's no longer is a diagnosis. Actually, although the fifth edition of the *Diagnostic and Statistical Manual of Mental Disorders* has chosen to exclude Asperger's, it must be noted that it is an American publication. To the best of our knowledge, the rest of the world still has permission to use the word *Asperger's.*

Insurance now uses the 10th revision of the *International Classification of Diseases* for billing, and there are different billing codes for autism and Asperger's. We will be using the words *Asperger's* and *ASD* pretty freely—not with an intention to exclude anyone but with the notion that many of the parents contributing to this book are describing children who are currently rather verbal.

Raising kids is hard; raising kids on the autism spectrum is extra hard and special. We are continually reminded of how fortunate we are to have the opportunity to work with such wonderful individuals.

These stories are amazing … grab some tissues!

Step I

The Beginning of Your Journey

one

"Hi. Intuition and I would like to schedule an appointment": Securing a Diagnosis

Autism is the common thread that pulls the next three stories together, but as you will see, each story is unique to the family. As you know, every child is different. The same holds true for children on the spectrum. Sometimes kids appear to be developing along a typical timeline, as evidenced by sitting, walking, and talking on schedule, only later to be diagnosed with autism. Other children exhibit warning flags from day one. Parents were asked to describe their experiences in securing an evaluation, how that process felt, and what they wish they had known at that time. We think you will find traces of your own story within those that follow.

Someday She Is Going to Rule the World

My daughter, Emily, was born in the middle of the night, screaming. She continued to scream most of her first night in the outside world. It was the same story each subsequent night. I snuggled and rocked this tiny baby every day and night, and she was simply inconsolable. At the time, we had no idea that this would be our life for the next three years.

Emily is my second born. Her older brother, Joshua, was 2½ when she arrived. Thankfully, he was a sweet, kind, and patient child because Emily cried constantly. It wasn't a typical baby cry—it was as if she was in pain from something we couldn't pinpoint.

I sensed a difference from the beginning. Emily was small and a terrible eater. She didn't laugh or giggle or think I was the funniest thing to ever walk the earth (my son, of course, thought I was hilarious).

She managed to pass her Ages and Stages Questionnaires (ASQ)—the forms at each well-child check to ensure her developmental milestones were met; but something was still not right. She cried all the time. I was nursing, so I cut food out of my diet, suspecting food intolerances. We rocked and walked, and I wore her in a sling, as I could never put her down. We tried reflux medications. Nothing soothed her or made her happy. She woke up constantly at night, almost every hour. The doctors said she would likely outgrow these issues. I wasn't so sure, but agreed to wait it out since she was still quite young. I managed to function on little to no sleep—keeping the house clean, cooking meals, and entertaining my wild and energetic toddler who seemed not to notice the 8 to 10 hours of screaming we coped with each day.

When Emily was 5 months, her older brother Joshua died unexpectedly. We were suddenly thrown into an uncharted new world of grief and sadness while dealing with an extremely unhappy, underweight, and sleep-deprived baby. Even though I wanted to stay in bed and pretend that everything was a horrible nightmare, I got up every day. I promised myself that no matter what, I would get out of bed, shower, eat, and take care of myself *and* Emily. My husband more or less bailed and threw himself into work and traveling. I was typically home with Emily alone. Since she cried from morning until night, I could not go to see friends, have play dates, or take her to baby classes. We lost many friends after Joshua's death, because they probably didn't know how to deal with our loss, nor did they know what to say. Apparently, they coped by never talking to us again. I spent most of my days trying to get enough nutrition into Emily to pass our monthly weight checks and the rest of the time trying not to physically harm her. I told myself every day that it was a good thing God gave her to our family, because I'm certain if she had been born into another family they would have shaken or hit her. She cried ALL DAY LONG. To cope with my grief, I was convinced there must have been a reason Joshua left our family: So that I could give Emily 100% of my attention.

At a year old, she still barely slept and was not feeding herself. This was mentally and physically draining—it took me hours every day to feed her. She hated food, hated eating, and hated sitting still to eat. She choked and gagged on anything with texture. We started feeding therapy, which taught her to self-feed. But this did not expand her repertoire of foods or increase how quickly she ate. She also had torticollis (a condition in which the head becomes persistently turned to one side, frequently paired with muscle spasms), which we treated with physical therapy. The therapy corrected the issue, and she continued along a fairly typical path, sitting up at 7 months, walking at 15 months, and speaking at least 50 words by a year. She spoke five- to seven-word sentences by 18 months. She could complete puzzles for a 4-year-old at age 2. For these reasons, our pediatrician was not overly concerned about her development. I wasn't concerned about her meeting these milestones either, as every child does things at her own pace; but I *was* concerned with her increasing tantrums and inability to cope with her environment.

The mere sight of another child would send her into a meltdown. We still could not go to music classes, gymnastics, or story time. Her meltdowns were the first indication that something was truly wrong. Ignore the behavior, and the child will get over it and forget what happened, right? This was not the case with Emily; these were not simple tantrums. She could cry and freak out for 2 hours over a hangnail. Or a bump in her sock. Or because I put her food on the wrong side of her plate. Because of her tantrums and the unpredictability of her behavior, we could not leave the house. We had just lost our oldest child, and now were housebound because we had a child who could not tolerate the outside world. It was lonely, frustrating, and sad. As someone who considers herself a "fixer," I was frustrated that I could not "fix" this problem. My friends could not relate to any of these issues, as their "typical" children did not do anything like what I was describing. We didn't do anything that normal families do—we didn't go out to eat or to the park; the thought of a vacation was laughable. No way. I couldn't even grocery shop with her. So taking her on an airplane or staying in a hotel was completely out of the realm of possibility.

When Emily was 18 months, I made an appointment with the child psychologist at our pediatrician's office. She was falling a little behind on her gross motor and social skills, but not enough to qualify for services. Unfortunately, at the time, our pediatrician's office did not have parents complete the Modified Checklist for Autism in Toddlers (M-CHAT). This is now routinely done at the 18-month well-child checkup. Had we filled this out for Emily, I believe things would have played out differently.

Emily cried and threw tantrums for half the day, sometimes the whole day. She complained that things were "too bright," "too loud," and "too much." She told us she couldn't sleep because the springs on her crib made noise when she moved. We got her a new bed, which, unfortunately, did not solve her sleep issues. We needed a break from our stressful life, but a babysitter was out of the question; Emily was too difficult and unpredictable. We were sleep-deprived and miserable.

I figured that the child psychologist could tell me whether she had autism or was merely an extremely difficult child. He was kind and empathetic, but only offered that she should start occupational therapy (OT) designed for children with sensory processing disorder. I was disappointed he didn't suggest testing her for autism but agreed that OT was a good place to start. I had looked at the checklists for autism, too; honestly, she didn't "fit" with the classical autism signs, so I didn't push it.

We began seeing a pediatric OT weekly. After a year of weekly OT with minimal behavior improvement, I made another appointment with the psychologist. Emily was passing her ASQs at her well-child checkups but still couldn't be in a room with another child without screaming, crying, or acting aggressively toward the child. She wasn't interested in potty training and refused to wear any clothing except for a sundress, even in winter. Thus, we were *still* bound to our house, except in extreme circumstances. Emily also refused most foods and was only willing to eat if we read a story to her while putting food in her mouth for her.

I explained our problems to Emily's pediatrician, this time stating that something more than sensory processing disorder seemed to be the cause. He agreed that testing her for autism was reasonable but recommended waiting until she was between the ages of 4 and 5. Emily was 2½, and I was pregnant with our third child. I couldn't even imagine continuing like this for another 2 to 3 years! That seemed insane. Plus, I *felt* a little insane. I hadn't slept or done anything fun outside the house for 2½ years. I nodded, took the information he gave me for our local children's hospital neuroscience department, and left. On the way home, I ignored his advice and called to make an appointment immediately. I also started calling any resource in town that offered therapy for children with autism. I asked everyone for suggestions on how to get her diagnosed and how to get her therapy. Unfortunately, Emily didn't "have" a diagnosis, so most places told me they couldn't help her. She was a highly verbal, affectionate, charming, and smart little girl … until she wasn't. At the end of that day, and every day, I felt incredibly discouraged.

I called Children's Hospital and was put through a triage screening process. They took my name and phone number, and a nurse called me back to see if I sounded like I needed to schedule an evaluation. I was told I would receive a packet in the mail to fill out, describing our concerns. Once I filled it out and returned it, we would be put on the waiting list for an appointment. Several weeks went by, and no packet arrived.

I made several follow-up calls but didn't receive anything. Once I realized I was never going to get it, I started calling around, trying to find a way to get an appointment. By this time, Emily was almost 3, and our lives were deteriorating. She often cried from morning to night, and again through the night. I had no idea how I was going to handle her and a newborn in just a few short weeks.

I finally found someone who gave me the name of an agency that works with Children's Hospital, but it was out of my insurance's network. I called and scheduled us an appointment – for 6 months later. As we were scheduling the appointment, the office manager told me our insurance would likely not cover the cost of testing if we scheduled through them. At this point, we would have paid anything to get answers and relief for our family. I finally felt that my luck was turning around. Six months seemed like forever, until we realized that the Children's Hospital waiting list is typically 12 to 18 months.

Around this time, we learned about early intervention (EI). I wondered why no one—not the pediatrician, occupational therapist, or psychologist—had ever mentioned EI. Looking back, I sense that this was primarily because Emily was not severely delayed in any area, and those who knew her best did not think she had the classic signs of autism. Unlike many children who are eventually diagnosed, Emily did not experience loss of abilities. In fact, she was years ahead on her communication skills. She qualified for in-home behavior and feeding therapy. Unfortunately, she aged out at 3 and received only 2 months of therapy. The EI team did not think she exhibited traits of autism. They referred me to the school district for further evaluation. This concerned me. She couldn't be in a room with another child without losing her mind, and I didn't feel good about sending her into a classroom with 15 other kids—for her sake or for that of the poor teacher. I felt she needed therapy to help her cope with her life and gain some skills and *then* go to school. I opted out of the testing at the district level and chose to wait for her evaluation.

The wait for our appointment felt like eternity, followed by an even longer evaluation process. The evaluation took 2 days. The first day we met with a developmental pediatrician for about two hours. The doctor spoke to us about Emily, in front of Emily. I didn't like that; she heard us talk about every criticism and struggle we had with her. She's smart and understood everything. The next day, teams from psychology, occupational therapy, physical therapy, and speech therapy evaluated her. While they evaluated her, we were asked questions about her skills and abilities in a separate room, which was video recorded. We could hear her screaming and crying—she cried for almost six hours straight. It broke my heart into a million tiny pieces. *Were we making a huge mistake?*

I didn't realize it in the moment, but the team was purposefully pushing her to identify her struggles. They had told us to bring snacks and expect a 4-hour appointment. Her appointment was 6 hours with an hour for lunch, which Emily refused to eat because we were in a new environment. She was potty-trained but had an accident during her evaluation because she was so worked up. After the evaluation was completed, we left with no idea how it went; we had to wait more than a month to receive the results.

The diagnosis was given to us in person. I think the teams were nervous, not sure of our potential reaction. To be honest, I was relieved and vindicated to find out she was on the spectrum—I was *right!* I finally felt that we could get help for her and that our lives might get better. I did have some negative feelings but was a little overwhelmed over what to do next.

We received written reports about 2 months later. Emily is very smart, and her verbal skills are phenomenal. She uses her communication skills to avoid tasks that are difficult. During the evaluation, she refused to do tasks asked of her and would not properly answer questions. As a result, they scored her as if she didn't know the answer or was unable to perform the requested skill. Therefore, the reports rated her below average to average in every area and said she would need significant support in all areas of her life, for the rest of her life. I felt this was not a true reflection of her abilities, but it made my head spin with questions: "Is she going to live with us forever?" "Can she go to college or get a real job?" "Will she lead a happy and independent life?"

Children's gave us the diagnosis and a big notebook full of information, but no one sat down to explain it to us. Medicaid waivers. Therapy recommendations. Various autism websites. When I asked where I should go for all these therapies, they had no answers. No one was there to guide the process of "What do I do now?" or "Where is the best place to get applied behavioral analysis (ABA—an intensive behavioral intervention for people with autism backed by research)?" We made a lot of mistakes and hit a lot of hurdles in getting all the recommended therapy in place. Dealing with insurance is an ongoing battle.

Having a child with behavior problems is difficult, particularly if there is no known reason for the behavior, as was the case with Emily before her diagnosis. Most outsiders (and some insiders, to be honest), thought that we needed to be firmer in our parenting, spank her, discipline her more, or that her behavior was somehow our fault.

Getting her diagnosed gave us something to tell people, including ourselves. We weren't doing it all wrong; we just didn't yet have the tools or skills to make it better.

Emily was 3½ when she was diagnosed. I wish I had followed my gut in the beginning and gotten her evaluated when I first noticed something was different, around 18 months. Additionally, I wish I had known about EI services. I truly believe that our quality of life would have been better, earlier, had she been diagnosed sooner.

Looking back, there were signs when she was very young, around 2 to 4 months. She lacked eye contact and never tried to get our attention or show us objects. She seldom smiled and refused to look at the camera for pictures. I tried to convince myself that this was just her personality. I don't hold ill will toward the experts involved in her care; they were only given snapshots of her life and depend on what we, as parents, give them. They all ultimately supported our decision to get Emily tested. I think some secretly thought we were wasting our time and money but nevertheless encouraged us to follow our instincts.

I am grateful that Emily was diagnosed. She now gets the therapy she needs. She is a thriving, happy, and joyful 5½-year-old little spitfire who sleeps soundly through the night. Our lives are completely different from 2 years ago: We can go out to dinner as a family; she is learning to read; she tells us she loves us, gives us hugs and kisses; and she even has a friend or two! Her meltdowns are few and far between.

It has been difficult personally, because doing anything for myself or socially is a challenge. Our days are filled with hours of therapy, leaving little time to nurture friendships other than with all the therapists who visit our house. My youngest, now 2½, also has motor and speech delays, so in addition to Emily's therapy, we have his therapy. It's difficult to find others who understand what we have gone through: We lost one child and have two kids with special needs. Most people don't have these issues and don't relate to us. We have to turn down birthday party invites, play dates, and other special events because of our hectic daily therapy life or to sensory overload concerns. Sadly, I believe we are considered to be bad friends, but mostly we are emotionally and physically exhausted from raising two kids with disabilities. It can be lonely and tiring keeping up with everything. I have to remind myself that it is a phase in our life and (hopefully) will not always be this way. It will be worth it, though, to see where our girl goes.

My Journey With Autism: In the Beginning

John was born almost 5 weeks early, after 3 weeks of total bed rest. My labor had begun at 32 weeks.

From the beginning, he was an absolute joy!

He was SO happy! … except when he wasn't. He was colicky. He was SO busy! … except when he wasn't. He was a late crawler, and didn't walk until after he was a year old.

He was SO talkative! … except when he wasn't. John stopped talking almost completely around 18 months. He had so many words before then, but regressed almost all the way back to "mama." I had surprisingly gotten pregnant again almost immediately and wondered if, somehow, having a baby brother is what had "changed" my child. Before, it was just us during the day, giggling and playing. But now, it was a very tired mommy and a baby brother. Had this caused him to stop being so chatty?

Was it that, at almost two years old, he had still never slept through the night?

Was it that he'd always been a little "sickly?" He was slightly asthmatic and seemed to catch viruses more easily than other children (we were in the pediatrician's office several times a month).

My husband's company had recently informed us that we were being relocated out of state. Who knows why John was struggling? Could John have felt the underlying tension of packing and selling the house?

When John was about two years old, I mentioned all these things to our pediatrician. She agreed that all these things could be factors but suggested not to worry about it for the time being. The next step was to get him into speech therapy. The pediatrician also recommended that we make an appointment with a new pediatrician as soon as we got settled in our new home. The stress of starting this process (insurance approval, etc.) was exacerbated by our impending move in just a month.

Four months later, we were all nestled into our new home, and settled into a routine. We had our first appointment with our new pediatrician. I gave her a copy of John's medical records, updated her on what our previous pediatrician's recommendation had been, and got the prescription for speech therapy, three times a week.

Recommendation: *Always* get copies of your child's medical records—from your OB/GYN and pediatrician as well as all specialists. I am truly surprised at how many times throughout the years we've had to provide records and/or answer huge questionnaires and I've had to refer back to the records myself.

By this point, I had discovered some things about John that made me say "hmm … that's different …" Everything was a routine and had to be done *exactly* the same way, every single day, every single time. If a change to the schedule was necessary, I had to let him know way in advance. If a change was made with no notice, we would have a full-on meltdown situation on our hands.

Incidentally, there is a huge difference between a tantrum and a meltdown. Tantrums are temporary and emotional. When John had a meltdown, it was not simply a temporary emotional overreaction. Something was desperately wrong! The fear and distress were tangible. The world had just fallen off its axis, and it seemed as if nothing would ever be OK again. Once he had a meltdown, nothing was right for most (if not all) of the rest of the day.

So many things would trigger a meltdown:

- Clothing issues: His shirt was the wrong color; his pants weren't soft (sweatpants); a button was missing from his shirt (they had to be full button-up shirts, fully buttoned up); the cuffs on his shirt sleeve didn't have that extra button closing the "peephole" by the cuff button. (Extra mommy stressor: How many shirts do you see for 2- to 4-year-olds that look like men's suit shirts?) Oh, and winter? In Chicago? No hat, no winter coat, no "glubs," no boots. He would choose to sit inside and look out the window at his brother and the neighbor kids sledding and building snowmen rather than put these things on. I was a "mean mommy" because I enforced the winter coat/boots/hat/gloves rule when it was below 25 degrees.

- Being in a new situation, especially one with lots of stimuli—noise, colors, motion, smells. (We tried to go to a professional baseball game once—ONCE. We tried to go to a *Veggie Tales Live Production* once—ONCE. We tried to go to a restaurant once—ONCE. You get the idea.)
- A change in schedule.
- Things done in the wrong order.
- If I took a wrong turn or didn't go the exact same way we always went when driving somewhere.

This last issue was what the speech therapist saw on the day she truly understood our daily life. Whenever John had a meltdown before his speech appointment, I could usually get him to calm down, but it always messed up the next few hours of his day. I would warn the therapist by saying, "He had a bit of a meltdown earlier," or "He's having a rough morning," so she would know today wasn't going to be as productive or he wouldn't be as responsive as expected.

On this particular day, I made a wrong turn on the way to John's appointment. There was a place where the road split; we always went to the right because it bypassed some traffic and extra lights. I missed the veer and was on the main road, but at the second light I turned right, then left onto the road we normally took.

UNHINGED!!!

My child came UNHINGED!!! In the backseat, while I was driving. I tried to talk him down, to show him landmarks to prove we were going the right way and that it would be OK. He was so upset I almost turned around and cancelled the appointment. As I was praying for strength and patience, I began to feel *very* strongly that I needed to keep going. I needed to show him that it was OK and that we would still get to where we were going. It was just a wrong turn! When we arrived, I told the therapist what had happened and asked her to at least take him back to show him that it was OK to make a wrong turn—it could still work out. Before the hour was up, she brought him back out to me. She was a wreck! (Thinking back on it, she probably looked like I looked all the time—completely frazzled, hair standing on end, awash in emotion.)

Then she said something I'll never forget, "Oh my God, Mrs. Doe—is this what he's like when you tell me he's had a rough morning ?!!"

To which I responded, "Well, yes, sometimes it's worse ... this was not really a bad one... ." She said, "I can't do anything with him! *Nothing!* I took him into our occupational therapist to see if she could help. We put him on this big swing, which seemed to help a bit (he'd always liked his baby swing), but there's something *really wrong* with John ... she wonders if he might have (whisper) *autism.* I said, "What's that?" (Dear Lord, was my baby going to die?!)

And so my journey into the world of spectrum disorders officially began.

After a discussion with my husband that night about the day's events and about the therapist's concerns, I felt lost and helpless. I didn't know what any of it meant, and neither did my husband. The next day I got a babysitter (no small feat), went to the public library, and began research. This was 2001–2002, so I didn't know anything about how to search online—not much of a World Wide Web back then. I made a list of books to buy and headed to a big chain bookstore. The first book I picked up detailed the *DSM-IV* diagnostic criteria (since revised in the *DSM-5*) for autism spectrum disorder, which doctors and psychologists use to diagnose autism and other mental disorders. I was shocked to discover that my child fulfilled almost all the criteria for autism.

The next step was to find a good doctor. I located a very well-known and highly respected specialist in Chicago who diagnosed and worked with kids with autism and Asperger's. But the wait to get in was more than 6 months. So I got us an appointment. Eight months later (the doctor had canceled our first appointment, and we had to wait another 2 months), we made the journey to our first appointment in downtown Chicago.

I recall feeling apprehensive, not just about the appointment, but also about the drive into the big city with my baby. We lived in the suburbs, and I had no idea how to get to Children's Hospital. Even with directions, it was horrible trying to find it. (Remember, John is in the back seat.) We finally found it, circled the block a few times to find a parking spot, and went up the stairs to the door closest to us—only to find it locked. Back down the stairs, down the block to the next door; inside to the waiting room. (*Shhh!* We must be super quiet in a hospital waiting room.) After waiting for about 40 minutes, we were ushered into a conference room with four people around a giant conference table. The people introduced themselves as interns or residents and PhD students. They informed me that the doctor wouldn't be there today, but here's a packet to fill out and bring back to your next appointment. Have a nice day. Wait. What?! Next appointment?

Two more months.

Two months later, John and I headed back downtown with the completed packet—all 23 pages of it. It had taken hours to complete. It asked questions about my history as a child, including details about my mother's pregnancies; my husband's history as a child, including details about his mother's pregnancies; my pre-pregnancy; my pregnancy; John's history as a newborn, baby, and toddler. Details even our parents didn't know were requested. Some of the questions were so rude and invasive, they brought tears to my eyes. But I did the best I could. This was for John.

For this next appointment, I knew where I was going.

John: "No Mommy! Wrong turn! Wrong turn, Mommy!"

Oh, Thank you, Jesus. A parking spot right in front!!

John, "No Mommy! Turn!!"

SERIOUSLY?! So I drove around the block; oh good, spot still open! "NO, Mommy, turn more!"

Around the block again—spot still open. "Now, John? Can Mommy park now? ... Please, please, pretty please?"

John, "Yes, Mommy, OK now.... (giggle) silly Mommy."

As we got out of the car to go inside, I tried to walk us, hand in hand, to the correct door. Nope. John guided me so sweetly and innocently up the wrong stairs, down the stairs, down the block to the correct door. My sweet baby...

After spending 45 minutes in the waiting room, we were called back into the boardroom, where again four people greeted us. I'm not sure if they were the same interns/residents and PhD students, because they didn't introduce themselves this time. Someone asked if I had the packet completed. When I assured them I did, indeed, have the packet, one of them walked down the table to get it from me and said to another, "Okay, go get her." After about 5 minutes, the doctor walked in, said, "I'm Dr. _____," and sat down at the far end of the table (near the students, interns, and residents) and picked up my packet. She opened it, and the others crowded around as she flipped quickly through it. She asked me a couple questions about my husband and me, pointed out a couple of things to the others in a whisper, then said, "Well. I don't think (flips open the file and studies it for a split second) John has autism. I think he's OCD." And with that, she stood up and walked out of the room! OK, thanks for coming.

I sobbed all the way home. At one point I had to pull the car over on the freeway because I was crying so hard. John was upset because I was upset but didn't understand what was going on. Neither did I. I had been seeing a psychologist for about a year, and the thought popped into my head to call her right then. So I did. And sobbed a message I don't know how she understood. She called back within a couple of minutes and told me to take John to the sitter and come right in to see her.

She was so upset when I told her what had happened and referred me to a nearby center that specialized in helping autistic families.

Despite the supposed expert who said John didn't have autism, I *knew* my son had it: I had read several books, including the *DSM-IV*. So I found another doctor. This doctor interacted with John and said, "Well, Mrs. Doe, John is definitely on the spectrum."

The things I learned:

- *You* know your child better than anyone else. If you think your child has an issue, keep seeing doctors until you find one who agrees with you and helps you figure it out.
- Doctors are just people. They make mistakes, too. Don't let your child slip through the cracks of the system just because one doctor doesn't see it.

- When it comes to your child, you, as a family member, *you* are the best advocate. Hopefully, throughout your journey, others will help you or you find someone who will, but you are the one there every day to fight for your child. It is exhausting, but YOU CAN DO IT!!!

- There are so many resources available now, but the best ones of all are the parents who have walked in your shoes. "Experts" can help, sure, but don't ever be afraid to talk to other parents and grandparents. These are the people who actually have been where you are. We are the ones who don't get to "go home" and leave it all behind us for a few hours. We are the ones who live it 24/7, just like you.

- Know your rights. That once felt intimidating to me, but it's not as hard as it sounds. And it's so much easier now to find the people and organizations who help. Know that the school systems are required by law to help your child get an education. They are required by law to give your child the necessary supports to aid in the success of your child. When you're told, "Well, Mrs. Doe, we do things a little differently here at _____ school," you have the RIGHT to say, "Well, we're going to have to develop the plan together now to ensure that you're doing the best you can for MY CHILD."

- At the beginning of each school year, I had a meeting with each teacher and at least one administrator in attendance. I handed out to each teacher a one-page sheet with John's picture at the top of the page and a quick little introduction letter with tips on how to help him achieve daily success, including how to spot a meltdown progression and how to help him head it off—and what to do if it didn't work. I made sure to include my cell number and e-mail and encouraged them to call or e-mail me with any questions or concerns. If John had a meltdown or stressor before school, I sent each staff member who interacted with him an e-mail warning that he'd had a rough morning. In short, I opened communication with each person who was part of John's day. I learned that every single one of his teachers through the years *wanted* to help John succeed! It was such an incredible revelation to know that I was not alone in my goals for John; sometimes it was a more involved process than others, but always a benefit for my son. Many teachers over the years told me afterward that they learned so much from John, and they thought they were better teachers for students on the spectrum because of their year with us.

- Learn what comforts your child in stressful situations. My son is *really* into animals and has stuffed animals from all over the world. He was much better if he could bring a "stuffed friend" to wherever we were going (interestingly, though, never to school). At about age 15, his father asked John to please leave his stuffed bright red dragon in the car when they went into the movie, thus beginning the slow process of being OK without his "friends" next to him. Now he carries around a small backpack-type string bag containing all sorts of things inside: his wallet, a multi-tool, a pencil and pen pouch and his journaling composition books, a book or magazine, and a few other things he seems to rotate. It's fine with me that this bag accompanies him everywhere; it quiets and settles him in a way that quiets and settles me.

- **Keep fighting ... Keep Advocating ... Keep Learning.**

My incredible son just turned 18. He is an Eagle Scout. He graduates from high school next month with a 3.35 GPA. He did dual-enrollment with the local community college his entire senior year, earning 15 credits to take to our state university in the fall. Although the challenges of dorm and campus life await him, I know he is ready for this chapter in his life.

I feel so blessed by this wonderful human who has taught me so much about, well, everything.

Let's Get to Work

My husband and I knew Leo wasn't like most babies from the day he was born. He slept for several hours at a time, to the point where the nurses told us to wake him so he could eat. Looking back, that was the start to our ever-evolving journey with Leo. As the first few days passed, more differences became evident. Something was just not quite right with our son. We could see that he didn't respond like other babies. He cried a lot, but when we held him, he would cry louder rather than being soothed. It seemed that he didn't want to be consoled by us. At about 10 days old, he was prescribed medication for acid reflux, and at 6 weeks he was diagnosed with colic. For the next 10 months, from 4 o'clock in the afternoon until about 9 at night, the house was filled with the sounds of a crying baby. As parents, we felt helpless and frustrated trying to comfort our son.

We continued to notice even more that things didn't seem right. As Leo progressed in age, we started to introduce cereals into his diet. Then, at around 8 months old, he refused to eat baby food, or anything else we tried to give him other than his bottle. By this time, still confused and frustrated, we knew we needed professional help. We took Leo to see an occupational therapist for the eating problems. This did seem to help temporarily, but at about 1½, he started refusing food again. Back to the bottle he went, and we were left once more with trying to supplement with formula and cereals.

In addition to his food refusal, we noticed other little oddities. Leo never crawled; he went from kicking, rolling over, and sitting up, to standing. He pulled himself up and started walking at about one year. Most of the time, Leo seemed very withdrawn and in his own world. There's a saying that babies talk with their eyes, but Leo didn't show any signs of doing that as a baby. At about one year old, I noticed that he played with his toys very differently from other toddlers. Leo displayed no imagination. He would line up all his toys, or stack them in a very calculated way. He often would stare at an overhead fan, seemingly mesmerized by its motion. Just after his first birthday he stopped making babbling baby noises and talking altogether. As parents we were progressively more confused and anxious to know why Leo behaved differently from other children his age.

We suspected Leo's mannerisms were some form of learning disability. We could not get anyone to validate or even acknowledge our concerns. Every time we brought up our concerns, the pediatricians would blow them off with, "I wouldn't be too worried. At this time, he's just a little behind." We felt increasingly frustrated and helpless.

Finally, when Leo was about 1½ we got his pediatrician's attention. Leo had two medical crises back to back. The first required multiple rounds of antibiotics. A few months later, he became very lethargic and unresponsive, and we rushed him to the ER. Leo's condition was critical, and because of his limited language skills, we were at a complete loss as to the source. We were left helpless for 3 days! As parents, we were inconsolable. I cannot tell you how horrible it is to have a nonverbal child who is that sick and cannot tell you anything.

Leo quickly recovered and was seen for follow-up with the pediatrician. The one good thing that came out of this was that the pediatrician had observed him closely for 4 days and agreed with us that something more was going on with Leo. He finally gave us a referral to Children's Hospital to be evaluated. They had a 6-month waitlist. So we waited. With nothing else we could do, my husband and I spent time looking into possible diagnoses Leo might receive. Very possibly, one of the most constructive things my husband and I did during the wait was to communicate with each other about what we were going to do after the evaluation.

Finally, the evaluation day arrived. After a long drive and 8 hours of waiting, a pediatrician and pediatric psychiatrist at Children's Hospital examined, assessed, and reviewed Leo's history.

Before we left that day, we had the diagnosis: *autism*. We were glad and relieved that we finally had answers and a diagnosis. When it was recommended that we have genetic testing done, we declined. That is what made sense to us. We did not want to play the blame game and were not planning on having any more children. So for us, genetic testing was not necessary.

As we walked out of the hospital that day, our only thought was, "Let's get to work." We knew the importance of early intervention and that we had already missed out on precious time. Immediately, we started a treatment plan for Leo: a speech pathologist/behaviorist twice a week; an occupational therapist once a week; and a physical therapist twice a month. We were very accepting of the diagnosis, but we refused to give up on Leo's quality of life.

For the first 6 months of therapy with the behaviorist, I cried every time the therapist left the house. I have a medical background, and knew I could trust her. I knew everything she did was necessary; but to see hand-over-hand techniques that Leo didn't like was hard. He just wanted to be left alone, but she did not allow that, and I knew we shouldn't either. She would tell me to change up his world daily and not let him get into a routine that would be hard to break. These kids are notorious for routines and obsessive-compulsive tendencies. As a result of Leo's need for routine, the therapy services have continued every week for the past 6 years. Even with the speech therapy early on, Leo continued to be nonverbal until he was 4½ years old.

As Leo reached preschool years, he was still a little behind the other kids his age. We continued with all of his therapies several times a week, as well as working with him at home. Toward the end his first year of preschool, Leo was still struggling with communication. We knew that if he progressed into kindergarten, he was going to fall behind, and that was not an option for him at the time. We met with his teacher, who arranged for Leo to continue one more year of preschool. Best move we could have done! One more year to learn and get caught up with his peers worked wonders.

Leo, now almost 8 years old, has mainstreamed into school! It is a victory for all of the early interventions and 5 days per week of therapy. He has blossomed into such a strong-minded, outspoken young man. He now speaks a thousand words a minute, or at least that is what it seems when he is telling us all about his latest toy and all the things it can do.

Each day has been an adventure. No matter how taxing it has been on us as the parents of a child with autism, we know that if we had not pushed when we did, or as hard as we did, Leo would not have progressed as much as he has. It's easy to sit back and take only what is given to you. But it is worth every ounce of energy, every tear, and every drop of blood to push yourself as a parent and get started as soon as possible.

The only part of the journey (thus far) that I would want to see changed is the medical profession's insisting on a child being 2 years old before evaluating for autism. Not all children can be diagnosed early on, but many (including mine) do show classic signs and symptoms and can be evaluated at an earlier age.

Summary

In sharing their stories, these families provide a glimpse into the diversity and complexity comprised in the simple word *autism.* The lessons are clear: The early warning signs vary greatly by child. The process of getting a referral can be difficult to navigate. Possibly most important, parents must be strong advocates for their children.

The red flags of autism have been well publicized. There are many resources to help identify these, including the Ages and Stages Questionnaire (agesandstages.com) and the Modified Checklist for Autism in Toddlers (M-CHAT). The experiences shared by the parents in this chapter demonstrate that sometimes the early signs are present at birth. At other times, parents start with an apparently healthy, well-rounded baby, when—*BAM!*—they find themselves raising a child on the autism spectrum. Both developmental pathways are real and frequent occurrences and are not indicative of personal shortcomings in parenting. The divergence in developmental pathways are wrinkles that can confuse and complicate the diagnostic process.

One thing is clear, regardless of when a child is diagnosed, parents play a pivotal role in the diagnostic process. You are your child's first and best advocate. You know your child better than any professional ever will. Please write lists, take notes, record videos, and share the information with your providers until you have been heard. Repeat the process until your child no longer needs your support—at which point, your child will be having children of his or her own and need your help with that adventure! Be. That. Parent.

Following are some resources that others have suggested:

- A long-standing, highly recommended source is Autism Speaks. This organization has partnered with JFK Partners to create a series of webinars. The following blog is specific for families engaging in the diagnostic process: autismspeaks.org/

blog/2014/01/24/delivering-feedback-families-how-can-we-teach-skill

- Find other families within your community who are raising children on the autism spectrum. They have the best insider knowledge about the process—local providers, the right karate instructor, and which summer camps accommodate kids on the spectrum.
- If you want to give back, share your knowledge and resources with people in the community: your teachers, physician, and therapists, among others.

two

"Got a minute? I have something to share with you.": Sharing the Diagnosis

Once their child has been diagnosed, parents are faced with a puzzle that comes in a series of questions: How will I tell my child? When will I tell my child? Do I have to tell my child? Who else needs to know? How can I do this and not mess up? Parents in this chapter were asked to ponder those exact questions, and they have shared their experiences with you.

We have seen parents struggle with the disclosure process, attempting to find the "right" way to tell their child. Turns out, the "right" way just happens to be as diverse as the children you are raising. For some families the disclosure process involves a 3-D model of the brain. Meanwhile, other parents are met with the reaction of a nonevent, best summarized by the quote, "Are we done yet? I'm hungry. Is it lunchtime?" There is no clear "right" or "wrong" time to disclose. You will know what is best for your child.

Am I the Only One?

It has been almost two years since we shared with Caleb his Asperger's diagnosis. It was in the summer after he finished fourth grade, and 2 years after he was diagnosed with Asperger's, ADHD, and a dash of anxiety. With every passing year, I could see Caleb struggling with daily challenges. Friendships didn't come easily for him, despite his best efforts; social situations were difficult to decode, and he was starting to feel somewhat different from the rest of the kids at school.

I felt that I owed Caleb an explanation; most importantly, I believed that he was ready. I would have preferred to do it sooner—maybe five or six months earlier—but my husband wasn't ready for that big step and questioned whether Caleb would be. Eventually, I started to feel dishonest by shielding Caleb from the truth. In my experience, honesty has helped my children feel respected and included. After a discussion with Caleb's therapist, a skilled psychologist he's been seeing since the Asperger's diagnosis, we felt Caleb was ready. Her quick and candid response implied that, in her opinion, he had been ready for a while. His psychiatrist also agreed. I convinced my husband that we had to tell Caleb that summer before school started, so he could have time to process it at his own pace without the pressures of a busy school schedule.

I scheduled an appointment with Caleb's therapist, e-mailing her in advance that the focus of the visit would be to tell Caleb that he has Asperger's. I also ordered several books for Caleb on Asperger's. He always has loved books and learned so well from reading and seeing information visually.

The psychologist and I sat down with Caleb and told him that he has Asperger's. We explained what it means, how his brain is wired differently, and we talked about the challenges and strengths that often come with Asperger's. We focused on the strengths that he has because of his Asperger's: his incredible memory, his attention to detail, his gift with math and numbers. We also gave him examples of famous people who have Asperger's and who have excelled in their fields despite some of the challenges that they had to overcome, especially those related to social skills.

It was emotionally difficult. It broke my heart seeing my 9-year-old son trying to make sense of it all. As a mother, my instinct is always to try to protect my children from harm and also from pain. But I couldn't make Caleb's Asperger's go away. I also didn't want to show him that I was too sad or worried about him. I tried to stay strong and calm. The therapist's matter-of-fact approach was so helpful for him. She kept the conversation at his level the whole time. We answered his questions as best as we could.

"*Am I the only one at school who has it?*" Caleb asked. It was his first question.

A few years later, I asked Caleb what his initial thoughts were right when he learned he was an Aspie. He said he wished we had told him earlier because for a while he felt that he was "a bit different but didn't understand why."

"I didn't understand what it meant. Once it was explained, it made me feel very mad, because I didn't want to be different," he recalled. "But it did help when I realized it came with other perks, like an awesome memory and intelligence."

Even though Caleb's brothers were still young (under 5) that summer, my husband and I told them that Caleb has Asperger's and explained what it meant. We kept it very simple, and again resorted to books. One book in particular, *What It Is to Be Me!: An Asperger Kid Book*, quickly became a favorite. They asked us, or Caleb, to read it to them every night for almost 2 weeks. I am convinced that the information helped my younger sons understand Caleb better and that it helped them be more patient and accepting of his quirks.

One day we were running late to pick up Caleb from practice. I worried that he would panic because I forgot to prepare him for the possibility that I might be late. As I was rushing to get to him, I asked my younger son if he thought Caleb would be very worried at that moment. "I wouldn't be worried. But I don't have Asperger's. So I'm not sure how Caleb is going to react," he replied.

Aside from our younger sons, we have shared Caleb's diagnosis with very few family members and friends. My husband is very private and very protective of Caleb's privacy. We also were aware that most of our family has never heard of Asperger's or autism spectrum disorders. We grew up overseas in a culture in which discussing mental health is mostly a societal taboo. It is a pressing issue that seldom receives the attention it deserves. Depression, for example, is either dismissed as a sign of a person's intentional negativity, or it is treated in secrecy. Not only is there little public awareness of mental health concerns, but there are very few resources for families and individuals. I feel so fortunate and grateful here to have access to outstanding psychiatrists, psychologists, speech pathologists, physical and occupational therapists, and so many groups and networks and resources for Caleb and for us as parents.

What we did share with close family members and friends is that Caleb sometimes struggles socially and therefore may at times seem uncomfortable in certain social situations. We told them he needs his space; he doesn't always like to look people in the eye; doesn't care for hugs and kisses; and he might take a while to open up. This mitigated any hurt feelings of family members and friends who would have otherwise taken offense to Caleb's unreturned hugs or attempts at conversations. It also helped them become more understanding and less judgmental of Caleb.

Disclosing Caleb's diagnosis with the school was a whole other journey. Initially, my husband and I were hesitant for many reasons. But eventually, we came to see that bringing the school to the table and involving them in the process would only benefit Caleb. The only way to do that was to be transparent—even though that meant having "Asperger's" on so many of Caleb's school records. It somehow made the diagnosis more official and more definite. But Caleb needed all the help that he could get, and the school had many resources that could assist with his needs. Without disclosing the diagnosis of Asperger's to the school, we couldn't secure an Individualized Education Program (IEP) for Caleb. Without an IEP, he couldn't receive the accommodations and assistance that he needed at school. There were classroom accommodations, including where he sat, where and how he could take tests, and do homework. There was weekly allocated time with a speech pathologist to help him with pragmatics and how to navigate working in groups. He also had a caseworker who regularly touched base with his teachers to make sure he was on track academically and socially. Together we became Team Caleb. That team was instrumental in helping Caleb grow, meet his potential, and get ready for middle school.

While at that elementary school, Caleb never shared his diagnosis with any of his classmates. We had explained to him that it was private, and that it was up to him to share—or not share—his diagnosis with any friends or classmates. One day in class, he mentioned in passing that he had Asperger's. He said one student asked, "What's Asperger's?" Another answered that it is "a contagious disease." That confused Caleb and made him feel sad and isolated. He had many questions for us that afternoon. I explained to him that many students probably don't know what Asperger's is, and the best that we can do is to educate them. I suggested that he give a presentation about it in class the following week. Caleb jumped on the idea, and his teacher was supportive. However, immediately after making a great PowerPoint presentation on Asperger's, Caleb changed his mind. He worried that some students wouldn't be respectful and supportive of his opening up about such a personal subject. To this day, Caleb says he hasn't shared his diagnosis with any friends.

"I like to keep it private because I don't want other people judging me," he explained.

If parents ever ask me for advice on how to share a diagnosis with a child, I would first recommend that you learn as much as possible about the diagnosis and how it affects your child. Books, workshops, events, TED Talks and support groups have been instrumental in my growth as a parent of an Aspie. Next, do it at the right time. Every child is different, but as a parent you will know when that right time is. When you do talk to your child, be open and candid about the diagnosis, and always focus on their strengths, communicating that you accept them for who they are.

Asperger's doesn't define my son. It's just a small part of who he is. I think it's also very important to build a support network. Some days are more challenging than others, and you might need to reach out for help or advice. Journaling is also important and helpful. This has been a long journey for us, and it is sometimes easy to forget the progress that Caleb has made and how far we have come as a family. This is our personal history and Caleb's, and journaling has helped document the important moments in it.

If I had to do it all over again, I wouldn't change the way we did it. I might have told him earlier, but I think it's better to be a little late than a little too early—assuming there is a perfect time. Caleb may have experienced deep, sad emotions when he found out about his diagnosis and will continue to occasionally feel that way throughout his life because of his Asperger's, but I learned that I can't protect him or shield him from his diagnosis. All I can do is help him understand himself, his strengths, and his weaknesses and teach him how to embrace it all and be proud of who he is.

In one of my favorite books on autism, *Following Ezra*, the dad (and author) summarized it best when he described how he felt after receiving his son's autism diagnosis:

> It has forced me to find and bring out something within myself.
> I feel full of love—for the boy who lines up the dinosaurs on the porch, for the child pretending to be Tigger in his bedroom, for the little one I carried and sang to in the first minutes of his life. My answer will never be to mourn. It will be to pour love on my son, to celebrate him, to understand, to support him, and to follow his lead. (Fields-Meyer, 2011, p. 23)

Resources

Fields-Meyer, T. (2011). *Following Ezra: What one father learned about Gumby, otters, autism and love from his extraordinary son.* New York, NY: New American Library.

Wine, A. (2005). *What it is to be me!: An Asperger kid book.* Fairdale, KY: Fairdale.

The Talk

How do you tell your child that she has autism? I was afraid to have this conversation with our daughter, believing it would scare Maddison or make her feel she was inferior to other kids. So, I put it off ... for years.

Our daughter was diagnosed with autism spectrum disorder in the first grade. Our hearts froze in fear and sorrow when we heard that word, and we struggled not to be angry with God over her condition. We had already been through so much with Maddison. She had seizures every day for the first 2 years of her life, did not speak until she was 3, would not make eye contact, and seemed behind in everything. When we told our family and friends about the diagnosis, they were not surprised. They all knew something was wrong. Almost everyone knew someone whose son, daughter, grandchild, or neighbor had

Asperger's or ADHD or autism. It explained so much about Maddison. There were many misperceptions about autism. I spent years educating people as to what autism was and was not, including that there were many levels of autism, from low- to high-functioning awareness.

I found that if I was straightforward about Maddison's autism diagnosis, people would be more open and forgiving of her social gaffes. We had several years where our daughter would ask people if they were a man or a woman. The usual cues of long or short hair didn't fit everyone. After explaining that Maddison had autism, they were very nice about these embarrassing moments. One woman laughed and said to me, "I knew I looked bad today!"

Over the years, I have found that more kids understand what it means when children are affected by autism, and many of them are compassionate—thanks, in part, to the increasing number of inclusion classes in school. Autism awareness and acceptance continues to grow with each generation. Unfortunately, there are bullies everywhere, and we have encountered a few of those.

Fast-forward to the present, where Maddison is now in the preteen years. We were at a loss as to how to proceed to tell her about her autism; fortunately, our choice to homeschool provided a platform to address this issue.

My husband and I made the decision to homeschool our daughter to try to catch her up to her peers academically, figuring that a one-on-one approach would help her learn more effectively. It was the wisest decision we ever made. At age 13, she was performing at a third-grade level. Within 7 months of homeschooling, Maddison went from not knowing her math facts, 1 through 10, to doing fifth-grade-level math! I was able to do things the teachers weren't allowed to do: Stay on one course until a topic was completely understood and mastered, reject poor work and make her do it over, impose consequences for bad behavior or poor attention (I charge Maddison a dollar for wasting my time, and she can earn it back for great penmanship), and take a "brain break" when she can't concentrate.

One of the things I do in homeschool is make up a new "facts quiz" every 2 weeks to enhance her awareness of the world. On this worksheet are questions that "regular" kids half her age would know:

where hamburger comes from, how many hours are in a day, what her dad does for a living, what "hold your horses" means, for example. These are things Maddison didn't know. We have conversations about these facts, and I thought this would be the perfect way to open a discussion about autism. One day, in her new facts quiz, I wrote the question: "Did you know that you have autism?" To this, she wrote the word "yes." That surprised me. Had the topic been addressed in school? I had no idea. Then the next question read, "Do you know what autism means?" Maddison wrote, "It means you are sad or mad." This meant she thought autism was bad behavior, not a condition you were born with. So if someone said she had autism it meant she was bad. Yes, the time was right for the talk!

I began our conversation with something familiar. "Do you remember Mrs. Jones's class? All the kids in that class have autism." After a brief discussion about what autism looked like in her classroom, our conversation resumed.

"That's right. Having autism means that your brain is wired in a different way from most people, and it can affect each child differently. Do you remember when you used to walk in circles a lot, put your toys in a line, or when you couldn't talk?" I asked her.

She shook her head no, then said with a face of disgust, "Don't say the word 'brain'—I don't like it."

"Well, the brain is where the wiring connects to help us think and to move our bodies, just like your robot toy with its electronic brain. Your brain is wired so that you have a super-sensitive nose and ears. You can smell things and hear things that I can't," I explained.

She looked proud. "Like Superman! And my eyes are good, too! I can read the words 'Atlantic Ocean' on the map across the room," Maddison announced.

"That's great! I wish I could see that well. But autism also sometimes makes you a little frightened of new things and makes you need special help with school and understanding things. That is why we are doing homeschool now," I said. I was almost holding my breath. Would she be overwhelmed by the information or sad that I said she was different from other children?

She looked bored. Clearly, this was not the dramatic revelation I thought it would be.

"When we teach you things over and over, your brain rewires and makes better connections," I said. "That's why we work so hard." I drew a picture on the chalkboard of a brain, getting ready to launch into a scientific discussion.

"Are we done yet? I'm hungry. Is it lunchtime?" Maddison asked. We broke for lunch, and she happily skipped down the stairs.

All this worry over that? I thought. Telling Maddison she had autism was like telling her she had blue eyes. She was not overwhelmed, saddened, or intimidated by it. Nor did she care. Perhaps in the future we will have that detailed, scientific discussion I had envisioned, but for now, the first talk had been broached with a successful outcome. It wasn't a big deal to her, so it shouldn't be such a big deal to me.

It Takes a Village

I've always been a pretty open person, so whether to share my son's diagnosis was never a question. Jayden, now 8 years old, was diagnosed with pervasive developmental disorder and sensory processing disorder at age 4, and then later diagnosed with autism spectrum disorder at 7.

I have been caring for children ever since I was 12 years old. I had studied autism briefly in an AP Psychology class and started my education to become a special education teacher, when Jayden was born. I then decided to focus on raising him full time. Although all this may have given me a small window into the world of autism, it never fully prepared me for what was to come.

The summer before Jayden turned 5, we had been visiting with my parents at their house. I don't recall what exactly set him off or why he was so angry and defiant. At the time, I assumed he was throwing a temper tantrum. And, honestly, I thought I was a bad mother because I couldn't get my son to comply with my directions. But my mother suggested I talk with my pediatrician to have him evaluated. She was wondering whether Jayden might have oppositional defiant disorder; he often tried to defy my directions or to do anything to make me mad. Knowing my mother had raised eight children and worked in an alternative high school, I trusted her when she suggested something else was going on with my son.

After receiving a diagnosis of autism, I (of course) shared the results with my mother. We were all relieved that we had an answer. Having a diagnosis gave us the information we needed to help Jayden. Knowing that he is on the spectrum informs the way we interact with him to suit his unique needs.

My dad said it had been obvious for some time that Jayden had problems socializing. He, too, was glad that there was a diagnosis to help me prepare for what I was facing and to research how to deal with it. To say the least, my parents have been very understanding and supportive.

I shared Jayden's diagnosis with my siblings as well. We were living near two of my sisters and their children, so there was a lot of interaction between them and Jayden. I also wanted to give my extended family the information and tools to help Jayden so that they could build a relationship with him. My youngest sister shared with me that she felt guilty upon hearing his diagnosis. She previously had expected him to act and behave a certain way, not knowing that it was often difficult for him. My older sister said it didn't surprise her after having observed Jayden for the previous 6 months, especially since her son is only 6 months younger than Jayden. Seeing the two of them together made the difference in development quite obvious. She noted that Jayden avoided eye contact and often refused a gift that she would bring home for him (gifts that even I thought he would enjoy). My family was accepting of the diagnosis and supportive of the changes we would need to make in how we approached his behavior and the relationships we would build with him.

But not everyone was as accepting of Jayden's diagnosis of autism spectrum disorder. At times I felt as if Jayden's behaviors were brushed off as "normal" when I knew they weren't normal. Jayden is quite high functioning, so people who were not around him very often did not see what we were able to see. Perhaps there was a little denial involved at times—even I "forget" Jayden has a neurological disorder, because he sometimes seems very similar to children his age. Then something will happen and catch my attention, which reminds me that Jayden sees the world differently, and I need to change the way I talk to him, explain things, and behave toward him to help him more fully understand the world around him.

Jayden's having an invisible disorder can be hard for me, because people tend to judge him as a typical child, not taking into consideration that his brain works differently from most people's brains. Some may question the diagnosis because Jayden looks and sometimes acts "normal." I often assumed that people were judging me negatively in how I raise my son, when they didn't know the reason for his behavior. But with time and patience, those who initially doubted have come to understand how autism affects Jayden and what approaches work best for him.

I shared Jayden's diagnosis with the school early on because he was having a very difficult time on the big bus. Our base school was 40 minutes from my house, and I was running an in-home day care at the time. I couldn't drive him to and from school, so the bus was the only option. As a kindergartener he sat at the front of the bus. Unfortunately, Jayden was placed next to another kindergartener in our neighborhood who was diagnosed with ADHD. Those two boys were like oil and water. This poor little boy assigned to sit next to Jayden was wild and loud. Jayden, with his sensory processing disorder, would become overwhelmed and would try to quiet the other boy by hitting him with his backpack. That year Jayden was suspended from the bus three times, and since I couldn't drive him to school, he missed school.

I started asking for an Individualized Education Program (IEP) shortly after getting his diagnoses because the negative behaviors were already present on the bus. I knew he needed a smaller environment. Our first few attempts to get an IEP were denied because the school kept saying "we need more data." This was infuriating to me. Basically, the school wanted proof that my son was failing before they would help him. Ultimately, I needed a lawyer to get the school to take me seriously. Jayden was given an IEP in the last month of his kindergarten year, which included special transportation to and from school. His experience riding to and from school went immediately from frightening, overwhelming, and stress-filled to calm and comfortable. Had I not told the school about his diagnoses, they would not have been able to give him the support he needed.

In terms of sharing the diagnosis, I was open with Jayden as well. I wanted to teach him to advocate for his own needs. To do so, he had to have as much information as possible about himself and about the diagnosis. I explained to him why we were going to the doctor. I told him that I was worried about why he was often angry and upset. I wanted to be able to help him feel comfortable, and I needed help, which is why the doctors wanted to talk to him.

We've always openly discussed autism in our household and around Jayden. He is present during all the discussions with the doctors, the therapists, and the school. Using this approach for the past 4 years has helped him gain a pretty good understanding of how autism affects him and why we do some of the things we do (i.e., therapy, routines, schedules, etc.). I've introduced him to other people living on the spectrum, including an adult who has been a great role model. This person has increased our optimism for what is possible for Jayden's future.

Finally, I chose to share his diagnosis with friends at church early on. Jayden often would melt down at church because of the noise and commotion. He had a hard time sitting still like the other children. Because my husband had to work, on many occasions I would be at church alone with three kids. If Jayden had a meltdown, I needed help watching after my other two children, then ages 2 and 1. For example, a few times Jayden would become upset because he didn't want to turn his phone off when church started. I would have to take the phone away, and he would scream, punch, and kick me. Then I would pick him up and carry him out of the chapel, leaving my two younger ones alone in the pew. I could do this because someone always moved over to sit with them until we returned. Fortunately, while Jayden was learning how to handle the church routine and I was learning how to help him, there was a woman at church who volunteered to be his "buddy." This amazing woman would give Jayden access to sensory breaks until he could calm down, as well as physically remove him from situations where he was a danger to himself or others during a meltdown.

I shared his diagnosis with my friends so they would have a better understanding of why he behaved the way he did, and why I had to practice extra patience to help him understand the world around him.

The decision of whether to disclose his diagnosis to him or to family and friends was never an issue. It seemed only natural to share his diagnosis. Autism is part of who he is, and I couldn't see not disclosing it to those closest to us. Being the parent of a child with special needs is hard, and I need the support of family and friends, as well as educational support. They say it takes a village to raise a child. I maintain this is even more true for a child with special needs. To disclose or not to disclose the diagnosis is a personal decision, not one that I can, or want to, make for another family. I will say that I am very grateful for all the love and support we have received thus far on our journey with autism.

Summary

No two individuals with autism are the same, and thus, your experience of sharing a diagnosis will be as diverse as the child you are raising. Although you may stress at length about sharing the diagnosis, there is no one right way to tell your child or others about this important aspect of their being. In fact, your hand may be forced at times. If anything, parents tell us they disclosed too late, but no family has ever referenced sharing a diagnosis with their child too early. Often families have told us that sharing a diagnosis brings a sense of relief and an explanation, much more than a burden. Children worry. Children frequently know something is different. An explanation goes a long, long way to understanding who they are and relieving their burden of worry.

Books can be helpful resources. Here are some books you may find useful:

- *Different Like Me,* by Jennifer Elder
- *Can I Tell You About Asperger Syndrome?,* by Jude Welton

- *The Survival Guide for Kids With Autism Spectrum Disorders (and Their Parents),* by Elizabeth Verdick
- *Socially Curious and Curiously Social,* by Michelle Garcia Winner and Pamela Crooke
- *The Journal of Best Practices: A Memoir of Marriage, Asperger Syndrome, and One Man's Quest to Be a Better Husband,* by David Finch

Two helpful websites include the following:

- socialthinking.com
- wrongplanet.net

Step II

The Middle of Your Journey

three

The Best Days

If you're raising a child on the spectrum, you already know the gifts that come with the diagnosis. Your child can memorize vast quantities of information. Your child may show unsurpassed empathy, love, and loyalty in ways you never envisioned. We asked parents to describe a best day with their child, including what made the day so special, what they learned as parents, and how this day perhaps changed their perspective on their child. As one of our authors points out, your child has the ability to bring you out of your comfort zone to change the way you live and to insist that you be present in the moment. Ultimately, this is how we were all meant to parent in the first place.

The Best Days Ever

"Nothing ever goes away until it has taught us what we need to know."
—Pema Chödrön

My father used to say, "The universe delivers its lessons in the most gentle way possible." He also said if we don't get a lesson the first time, the universe is happy to hit us over the head.

I'll admit: I've been hit over the head a lot. I was a stubborn kid, an impulsive and headstrong teenager. I like to think I've let some of my stubbornness go as an adult, but that probably depends on whom you ask. As far as early "gentle" lessons from the universe regarding my "it's my way or the highway attitude," I don't remember them. I was probably too stubborn to connect the dots.

Perhaps the most enduring lesson arrived in adulthood. My first child was born when I was 33 years old. I'd waited longer than most people I knew to become a mother, mainly because I wanted to "do it right." I wanted to be ready. I wanted to have traveled. I wanted to have experience with things that I knew would be difficult if I had young children in my 20s. So by the time I was ready to become a mom, I had a lot of expectations about how things would go. I was going to be a perfect mom. And I was going to have a perfect kid. It was going to rock.

I'd read all the baby books. Talked to my friends who were mothers. I'd investigated the various teaching methods at preschools, and knew where I'd send my son when he was ready. I had a plan. And then my son was born. I remember the doctors placing him in my arms and falling in love with him right away.

But what happened over the next few months and years was not in my playbook. My son took a long time to sit up. He took longer to crawl. He seldom made eye contact with me. He didn't coo, and at 18 months of age, did not say any words. I began to worry—a lot. Regular pediatric visits came and went, and doctors assured me he was fine. But I knew he was not fine. My gut told me something was wrong.

At age 2, he was diagnosed as "at risk" for an autism spectrum disorder. I remember the awful fluorescent lights in the doctor's office, the shot of panic as she told me the diagnosis. I remember the tears as I repeatedly asked her, "What does this mean?" and, "Will he be OK?" and the disbelief when she said gently, "It is too soon to know."

It would be another year before we had the official diagnosis of autism spectrum disorder. I was in a panic for the year leading up to the official diagnosis—coordinating behavior therapy sessions, speech therapy sessions, reading everything I could on autism, and learning behavior modification techniques so that I could support my son's recovery. I was determined he would recover. I was determined he would speak. Determined that he would be like every other kid. Accepting the diagnosis was the furthest thing from my mind. I was not going to accept autism; I was going to beat it.

And in a way, we did beat it—we won. My son is now 9 years old and in a typical classroom with his typical peers; a layperson would never suspect that there ever was a diagnosis. And so I justified my stubbornness and my obsessive-compulsive management of therapy sessions and my own high expectations because we "beat" this thing called autism. What I was missing, though, while I was running therapy sessions and behavior support services like a mafia boss, was happiness. I was so focused on the outcome that every day was a stress-packed, exhausting, miserable mission. Not that I was aware of this at the time—I was doing the best I could. I was fighting for my son. I was acting out of a love that, more than anything, wanted to ensure that he would be OK. But the days? The days were long. The days were worry-filled. The days took a toll on my marriage and a toll on my health. I became depressed, my temper short.

I recall one day, as I was rushing through the grocery store with my 2-year-old son in the shopping cart, a woman looked down at my son and smiled and said, "Remember these days, they are the best—and they go by too fast." I felt my face get hot and the welling up of tears and I thought to myself: If she only knew—these days are not going by fast. These days are moving at a painfully slow crawl; these days feel as if they will never end. These days may kill me. But you can't say that to a kind stranger in the cereal aisle. I nodded, tried to smile, and whisked by her as I tried not to cry in the store. And when I got home, I lay on the bed and wondered why. Why did everyone else get to have the best days? It wasn't fair. *We* should be having best days. But instead I was running myself ragged. I'd lost my sense of humor. I believed that we would never have a best day; I'd lost it.

I then had a second son. He was born extremely premature, but from all appearances, was not on the autism spectrum. And then things began to change. Something was not right. My younger son began to exhibit the typical "warning signs" for autism. I took him to doctors and was told he was fine. I was told his developmental delays were a result of his premature birth. I was told by clinical child psychologists and certified behaviorists that he was not on the autism spectrum.

So here I was, a mom with two kids. One child had a diagnosis I'd never really accepted, the other a diagnosis I couldn't quite believe.

And as my younger son grew up, the warning signs of autism became more prominent. His social language was delayed, he fixated on things, and he struggled to regulate his emotions. He was in trouble at home, in trouble at school. I didn't know what to do. Surely we would not get the same news twice. I didn't have the energy to pursue a full-on crusade to beat whatever was ailing my younger son. I decided those were days I could no longer bear. So I became quiet. I tried to just live in the days, not to change them. I tried to just observe the days. To watch, to see if there was anything they could show me. And I hoped for a different way.

We found another doctor. I brought my younger son to him, and the evaluations began. Interviews began. Developmental histories began. I recounted my older son's diagnosis and early intervention, for which I am forever grateful. I recounted my second son's difficult birth and all the doctors who said he was fine. The new doctor talked to my husband and me and spent time with my son. He tested my son. I waited. I cried to my husband. He told me, with utter compassion and love, "Whatever it is, we will deal with it." And I chose to believe him. Because there had to be another way; there had to be a way to find peace in our days.

One day my husband looked at me as I was rushing off with my son to a behavior therapy appointment and said to me, "What is the goal of all of this? Is it for him to be normal? Because normal is overrated. And if you want to know something, I don't want him to be normal. I want him to be the best version of himself he can be."

It took me a while to process what my husband said to me. But something happened when I did: I thought to myself, "What if? What if I stopped wishing my son was like every other kid on the block? What if I just let my expectations go? What if, instead of worrying about whether he'd be OK, I started enjoying his quirky, smart, beautiful manner? What if I stopped worrying about what other people thought? What would happen?" I decided to try.

Shortly thereafter, my husband and I went to the new doctor to receive my younger son's diagnosis. Before the appointment, I forgave myself for not accepting my first child's diagnosis. I forgave myself for thinking my mission was to "fix" him and that while I was so grateful for where we were, I openly accepted anything that was to come. I repeated this to myself, to my spouse, to the universe. I had faith that the universe had heard me.

And our days began to change. My kids smiled more. I smiled more. I found myself laughing for the first time in years. I decided to embrace the days, no matter what. The diagnosis would not define our days. Love would define our days. Compassion would define our days. Hope would define our days.

During that appointment, my second child was diagnosed with autism. I still believe the universe heard me. And in quiet moments, I can hear its gentle, loving, reply: These are your best days, my dear, and you are so, so, very blessed.

Reference

Chödrön, P. (2000). *When things fall apart: Heart advice for difficult times.* Boulder, CO: Shambhala.

Reality Calling

The best day with my 20-year-old? Well, *every* day, of course. No, really. My kid is amazing, and not a day goes by that he doesn't teach me something, release me from my comfort zone, and show me the depth of his feelings.

When we started on this autism journey he couldn't speak, didn't know how to play, had no social or self-help skills, and basically didn't stop for 16 hours a day. So, now, being able to interact with this intelligent, engaging, matter-of-fact, funny guy makes every day with him the best.

I am no shrinking violet. Before becoming a stay-at-home mother, I had a successful career in sales. I am convinced that Michael came into my life to bring me way out of my comfort zone. Having to advocate for him changed me. I found strength where I never knew any existed. In many ways, he helped me to find my way just as I did for him.

Michael was diagnosed in 1998 when he was 2½. At that time, there wasn't a lot of information out there about autism. Some of what I read had to do with "refrigerator mothers." Thank goodness I was confident enough in my parenting abilities at that point to know that I did not cause my child's autism. Back then, there weren't any websites, or blogs, or Facebook pages where parents could share their challenges, joys, and deepest fears. We were pretty much on our own.

While Michael responded very well to the immediate speech and occupational therapies he received, and also to our constant carry-over at home, we felt he needed more. Three months after his diagnosis, I am grateful to have read about applied behavioral analysis. Programming would target every area of his development. Somehow I just felt that it was what he needed to excel. This type of programming did not exist in our very rural part of the state, but I couldn't let that stop me. I found a behavior analyst 6 hours away, and she helped me to lobby our state's early intervention agency. Ours became the in-home pilot program in our area, and I became Michael's first teacher after intensive training. We autism families will do just about anything for our kids.

From the start, we reveled in every one of Michael's accomplishments. He said "O" for video; we cheered! When I told him one morning about the occupational therapist we were going to see, he immediately ran to the refrigerator, grabbed the picture of his other therapist, and brought it to me. No words needed but message received: "I want to see this woman!" I went nuts! We learned very early on that every bit of progress was epic. Every day was momentous.

Now Michael has a vast and rich vocabulary. He masterfully volunteers at two different libraries 10 hours a week and thoroughly and efficiently performs cleaning tasks three times a week at my husband's office. He could easily be a master builder with LEGO® toys. He can compose a professional and expressive letter or e-mail (especially to someone who will be able to connect him to beloved train paraphernalia). About 5 years ago, he even reached his goal of losing 60 pounds. Michael still struggles with overwhelming anxiety and impulsivity. There is a disconnect between what he believes are legitimate life goals and what is feasible, taking into account his difficulty with social interactions and appropriateness. Thus, while I will always say that the best day with my son is every day, it doesn't mean that every day is easy.

He craves independence, but is easily derailed by unpredictable situations or by people's reactions. He must have someone close by at all times to intervene, if necessary. Over the past several years, texting between us has played a huge part in his feeling in charge of his own life when he's volunteering, allowing me to keep my distance but still being able to check in to be sure he's OK. I don't exaggerate when I say that his iPhone has changed his life. So, I guess if we really had to pinpoint one best day, it was when he decided he wanted this phone.

I'm probably the only mother on the face of the planet who does not say to her kid, "Put away that phone." I'm *thrilled* to see Michael's eyes down, scanning his screen and doing what almost every other 20-year-old in the world is doing! In fact, it took us more than a year to convince him that he should have a phone.

It's an understatement to say that our guy is a creature of habit. Just the change of seasons used to elicit massive anxiety attacks. Sameness keeps his life, his entire being, calm. He still has a Game Boy (which he's had since his ninth birthday). We bought him a Nintendo DS many years later so that he could upgrade. He thanked us, but made us return it. He was content with his Game Boy. He recently purchased a new screen for it. (Yes, you can still find these.) After he finished installing it, he declared, "Look. Just like new."

When Michael was almost 17, we started to plant the seed of making a phone part of his life. Our desire for him to have it was primarily to increase his independence and to reinforce his safety. We wanted him to be able to go to a different aisle of the store without one of us hovering near him all the time. If we ever got separated from him, we needed a way for him to connect with us and us with him (other than our tried-and-true method of screaming his name while running frantically to every aisle we think he might be in). He wanted no part of it. "No, thank you. I'll be fine."

Then his brother, Christopher, got an iPhone. Michael loves his big brother, but technology always seems to bring their interactions to a whole new "cool" level. Just as Christopher had gone to Michael for his photography and videography expertise when setting up his business, so Christopher became the go-to guy for Michael's iPhone questions. He started to read up on apps and all the possibilities that came with them. I think the day that changed his entire outlook was when he saw Christopher looking online for a better price on an item while we were standing in the aisle of a store. For a kid who loves facts and information, the possibility of having the Internet at his fingertips 24/7 was the Holy Grail.

Shortly after his high school graduation in 2013, Michael came to us and said, "I think I'm ready for a phone."

You might recall I said that one of the reasons we wanted him to have a phone in the first place was to become more independent. How is this for being self-sufficient: Several weeks after he bought his phone, he and I were on a trip. We had stopped into a bookstore and were standing in line to pay. I saw him looking at a rack of gift cards. He chose a $50 iTunes card, turned to me and said, "I'm using my own money to buy this so that I can get apps for my phone."

One of his *many* apps scans food nutrition labels. For the past 2½ years, he has maintained his 60-pound weight loss. I can't tell you how many people have asked him his secret. "Eat less. Exercise more," is always his matter-of-fact answer. He achieved this with a very limited diet due to sensory difficulties. It appears that the apps keep him on track as well.

Periodically, he informs me that he needs to buy another iTunes card to put on his account. He doesn't drive (yet—that will be another story for another milestone, I'm sure), so I take him to the store, but he completes the purchases entirely on his own. I'm thrilled that he stands in line, waits his turn, carries on a polite conversation with the cashier, produces his payment, and counts to make sure he's received exact change. This took so many years for him to learn. Now he's using these skills to buy something that makes his life enjoyable and useful. It makes me giddy!

While I sometimes feel guilty for some of the traits my kid inherited from me (or the behaviors he adopted by watching me) I am quite proud that he is a bargain hunter. Recently, he, his dad, and I were looking for a replacement screen for his electric shaver. Dad and I were ready to buy a whole new shaver (same exact model because we know our kid), because the replacement screen and blades were almost as expensive. Have I mentioned how Michael likes things the same? He wanted no part of the new shaver and was ready to make his case. He got on his iPhone, searched replacement screen/blade kits, and found one for half the cost with free shipping on Amazon. We ordered it when we got home. That's my boy!

While he has a massive vocabulary and is very articulate, don't call him up expecting just to chat. He doesn't really get the point of small talk and therefore hates it. Politely, but in no uncertain terms, he also will tell a caller just that. Fortunately, his circle of callers includes those who already know this. Basically, tell him why you're calling, give him the information or share whatever funny anecdote you want to tell him, and get off the phone. It's perfectly OK for him to explain, in great detail, something that he wants to tell you, but don't bore him with your small talk. You've been warned.

As my son grows older and I have time to reflect on his many milestones and accomplishments—from that first "O" to our now frequent phone conversations—I am swept with the sense that each day gives us reason to celebrate. Truly, every day is the best day with my son.

Our Best Day

The best day with our son, Arlo, occurred during an unexpectedly long hike in the Pacific Northwest. The day started like most vacation days, with a hearty breakfast and high hopes. We planned a moderate morning hike, gathered our supplies, went to the trailhead, and then our family of five headed off into the forest.

Right from the first giant squishy black slug we met near the trailhead, everything clicked.

Over the course of the next 2 hours, we watched Arlo immerse himself in the world of the Pacific Northwest rainforest. He studied the slugs and snails, keeping track of all their similarities and differences, and made connections with vivid memories of past trips. He amazed us all with his insights and powers of recollection. While I remember little about the giant banana slug we had seen a few years earlier, Arlo could answer every slug question his brothers threw at him, and then could relate it to the new discoveries he was making on our hike, mesmerizing his bug-savvy brothers.

As each of the creatures along the trail sparked his interest and imagination, he transformed before us into a passionate, charismatic educator. The whole family, and especially his two brothers, got to see Arlo in a whole new light. We were learning from him, and he was responding to our enthusiasm by finding more things he knew we'd enjoy. When we crossed paths with a pair of hikers later in the journey, Arlo confidently engaged in conversation with them about the trail. It was a surprisingly balanced conversation, he showing interest in what they had to say, while offering observations of his own.

After 2 hours of hiking on various offshoot trails, our adventure could have ended there and it would have been a great day. Arlo's body is more sensitive to his surroundings than the rest of us, and he's the first one to feel too hot, too cold, too sweaty, too itchy, too much wind, too much noise, and the list goes on. But today was different, as if he had discovered the strengths that come from being a highly sensitive person. He enjoyed standing out and taking advantage of this quirk in his brain's wiring. He has an amazing ability to spot any type of movement in his entire field of vision and always has been the first to see the smallest bugs, the slowest slugs, the fastest lizard, and the most obscured birds with their subtle, quick head movements. We saw more details and wildlife than ever, thanks to Arlo, the perfect nature guide. Still, his younger brother needed a rest even as Arlo persuaded us that there were more discoveries ahead on the trails.

After finding a picnic area for our rest, Arlo came across a stump to serve as a movable chair and got going on a new project. He had been examining structures along the hike and decided he was going to investigate how to build "like nature." He got to work experimenting with various combinations and compositions of rocks, leaves, twigs, moss, and more. Some of his techniques failed, others were solid, but none was random. We expected to simply see repeats of one of his many LEGO® brick-building sessions from home, but we were very wrong. Arlo started combining structures we had seen along the trail with new, detailed designs that used the materials in ways we never had seen. As we watched it all evolve; Arlo was relaxed, having fun, and really interested in learning about how these systems could work together.

During the hour-long hike back to the car, so much was alive in Arlo's mind. He stopped in awe of a stunning spider web. The web was large and well shaped, with dew and light, making it stand out against the backdrop of the dense forest. After pointing it out to us and noting its beauty, he examined its construction to see how a spider could create the large web. It was a day of discovery for everyone. Arlo discovered a growing interest in nature, and our family discovered that we had an excellent, creative, and observant trail guide among us. The great memories from this day return often, whether we're walking in the neighborhood, hiking new trails on vacation, or catching a glimpse of the complexities and aesthetics of a spider web in a piece of art that he created in school.

This amazing hike afforded us the opportunity to learn a lot about our son and about nature. When Arlo takes an interest, he has a unique ability to bring things even more alive. We came away from our day with a deeper appreciation and understanding of the forest, and we experienced so much more because Arlo exposed it for us.

More importantly, though, it gave us new positive insight into our son, his passions, and his brain. I felt as though we got a glimpse of the future, when all of the processing comes together and he can be truly outstanding in a field of interest. We witnessed great examples of how he might eventually apply his current hobbies (such as constructing LEGO® creations and building things in general) both into real-world work and into better relationships with other people. He had natural give-and-take conversations with the people we encountered on the trail. His enthusiasm was contagious, and he was relaxed yet helpful with his brothers.

We saw evidence that Arlo's brain has the capacity to take in a huge amount of new information, organize it, process it, apply it, and then share it. After the way we had seen him struggle through the previous school year, this was thrilling for us. Seeing these elements all come together successfully spoke volumes about how his mind works. An added bonus for the day was watching Arlo subconsciously learn to push past some of his sensory issues. We still deal a lot with sensory issues throughout most days, but we have hope for the future.

Never before had we recognized these elements of his personality jell in such a thorough manner. We had seen glimpses of it through work with therapists and at school, but Arlo was guided and it came out in small chunks. It is much different seeing his brain work as spontaneously as it did on that day, and it opened up a whole new perspective on our son and the way he sees the world. From various assessments, we were aware of Arlo's strengths and weaknesses. But the day of the hike was the first time that we got a bigger, fuller picture of how these strengths and weaknesses will intersect to create a complete, well-rounded person.

Arlo showed us expanded interconnections in nature that we hadn't seen ourselves, so from that perspective, his observations and experiments presented information we never had accessed on our own! His combinations of conventional and unconventional techniques, using objects found in nature at our rest stop, showed us new possibilities that come from raising an original thinker. It is exciting.

This outstanding hike changed our perspective on how an Asperger's brain adapts and molds strengths and weaknesses together in the most effective manner for that person, and that person only. Some activities that seem ill suited for Arlo's personality or disposition can turn into wonderful opportunities for him to approach problem solving in his own, unique way, and surprise us. Having great memories from a regular day, doing a family activity that we love, gives us a great reminder when we are stressed and getting lost in the everyday ups and downs of school, peer relations, and seemingly inflexible thinking. That nature hike with Arlo created an unexpected trail that has led us to a better understanding of our curious, intelligent, *fascinating* son.

Summary

Kids with autism bring unique strengths to the table. As a parent, you have the opportunity to witness amazing feats of literal language coupled with innate, insatiable curiosity about a topic. If you are open to it, your child will offer you a different lens with which to view the world. You and your child will discover distinctive personal resources, and these may emerge in unexpected situations, such as seeing a spider web on an amazing hike.

You may find that you celebrate other things parents take for granted. One family's constant reminder, "Put your phone down," is another family's celebration that they are connecting to others by texting. Your beloved children express empathy, love, and honesty in a way the rest of the world doesn't anticipate.

No websites or other resources are recommended here. We simply encourage you to recognize and nurture your child's strengths and passions. Temple Grandin, for example, is well known for encouraging people to turn their passions and special talents into a career.

four

Wine Won't Solve This: The Harder Days

Spoiler alert: crying ahead! Raising a child is hard. This chapter cuts to the core of the choices we make as parents and the people we become as a result. Parents were asked to describe the more difficult aspects of raising a child on the autism spectrum, including what made a certain day so challenging, what they learned from it, and would they give up that painful day if they also had to lose the lesson it taught them about how to better understand their child's experience.

The Lesser of Two Evils

Even though it was the lesser of two evils, and it may have saved his life, it was still evil, and no amount of time, therapy, or wine will completely erase the guilt that I feel about it.

I believe I am fortunate in that I do not carry a great deal of guilt regarding Jacob. I took no risks during my pregnancy. My stress was that of the pregnant mother of a toddler and a family trying to figure out how to have the baby affordably when our insurance didn't cover it— nothing uncommon. There was no turning point in his development as a child that I can point to and say, "That's what caused autism." If there had been, my husband, Andrew, and I never would have gotten over it. We'd soldier on, but we'd carry that burden heavy and hard.

When Jacob was 3½, I took a job abroad and moved my two sons and husband from the United States to our new home away from home. Jacob's older brother, Noah, was 5½.

Jacob was a flight risk from the moment he learned to roll over, and once he learned to run, he had to be kept close. A lot of toddlers are like this. Noah had taken his first tentative steps, and then only ran for 8 months. *But* he listened when we explained safety, and he understood the sound of danger in my voice. He was aware of cars on the road and treated them with respect. If a car driving by us made a loud noise, Noah ran away from it. Jacob ran toward it.

I learned how to do just about everything outside the house while holding Jacob's hand (or his coat collar or hood if he wouldn't hold my hand). Chase was his favorite game, and he had no understanding of when it was an appropriate time and when it was not. No amount of explaining, begging, warning, or demanding made a difference. If we were someplace other than in the house or the fenced yard, he was going to force me to chase him.

People used to stare. Some even would comment: "You need to control that child," and, "You need to discipline him more," were the most common admonishments. These came from strangers and, more painfully, from friends. We started applied behavioral analysis (ABA) therapy when he was a little more than 2½ years old. (ABA involves a series of tasks, like responding to one's name, and then being provided with meaningful rewards.) We worked on compliance. We worked on responding to me when I called him, when I was close and from a distance. I believe Jacob ran because his little body was so bombarded with stimuli that he *had* to run. His occupational therapist (OT) agreed that he was ruled by his sensory needs. Following the instructions of his OT, we brushed his limbs and compressed his joints; we used an exercise ball; we spun him; we hung him upside down; we bought a mini-trampoline; Grandma and Grandpa bought a big trampoline; a friend made a heavy blanket for us; we squeezed him in a bean bag; we hugged hard. And he still ran.

We had few options when we moved and had to rent a flat on the second floor with 12 slots of parking shared among more than 25 condos. When we managed to get one of the slots, (probably fewer than 10 times in the 8 months that we lived there), we celebrated. Usually, we had to park on the street. The streets always had cars parked on both sides, right up to the corners, even *on* the corners, and as close to driveways as possible. There were no bike lanes. Cars pulling out of driveways had to pull past the sidewalk, then past the parked cars, and then nose into the road for the driver to be able to see the traffic. Large delivery trucks frequented the road, as did fast, law-defying motorcycles. We were surrounded by people with busy lives, with places to be, and, as a result, people came out of their driveways without caution. I knew it was a dangerous situation and that I had to be on high alert any time we were on the sidewalk.

All of this was happening in the opposite way that it did back in the United States. In our new home, drivers were on the right side of the car, and oncoming traffic came from the right side. I had to watch Noah far more carefully than I had in years. He realized the change in the flow of traffic quickly enough, but I worried about how old habits can become reflexive when we are fearful or stressed.

When I arrived home from work with the kids, Jacob was routinely kept locked in the car until I could get out, gather our things and square myself. Noah stayed in the car to keep Jacob there by example. Then I'd let Noah get out so Jacob knew which side to use. He often would climb over Jacob, depending on which car door was closest to the curb. (Cars were allowed to park facing either direction there, and I always chose the spot closest to our home.) Noah would take Jacob's hand while Jacob was still in the car and let him out. Sometimes, he'd have to physically restrain Jacob if I wasn't able to get there quickly enough. Jacob thought it was great fun to try to get out of the car without holding my hand or to get free and run.

It was inevitable.

I worked at a private, international school and dressed in smart clothes, almost always in heels. Heels that day. I had my laptop slung over one shoulder, my purse on the other shoulder, and the pictures Jacob had colored that day plus my keys in one hand. As I shut my car door, he slipped out of my grip and was gone with a giggle and a squeal of delight.

Noah was after him immediately, as was I, but I knew instantly that we wouldn't catch him before he got to the first intersection. He was only steps away from the first driveway and could at any instant veer off into the road just for fun. I heard large trucks behind us and saw a city bus ahead. In that instant, weighing my options, I slid my handbag off my shoulder, and threw it at him. It hit him squarely in the back and sent him sprawling on his hands and knees. His brother stopped dead and turned to look at me with nothing short of terror on his face.

As an aside, if I don't carry a tremendous amount of guilt about Jacob, I do carry considerable guilt and concern regarding Noah. He's been there through my very worst moments, usually watching with wide-eyed disbelief. I can't erase those moments. I can't give him back the lost innocence. He's growing up knowing that his mom has flaws. Big ones. She shouts when she's tired and tested. She curses when things get to be too much. She cries, and sometimes she intentionally hurts his little brother. Does Noah think that I did that to *him* before he was old enough to remember? We have thrown all of our resources, time, and energy into Jacob, but what of Noah? This keeps my husband and me awake at night. What about the siblings of all those children out there with autism? Who's watching out for them? I used to feel that I lost Jacob when we got his diagnosis. Am I going to lose Noah as well? When we think he is happily playing on his tablet while we attend to Jacob, is he instead wondering why his parents don't love him as much as they love Jacob? Does the patience that he portrays mask resentment or sorrow? Naturally, all this ran through my mind as I saw the terror on Noah's face. And my legs just kept running.

I never stopped running, just swooped Noah into my arms and then went to my knees beside Jacob, who was gathering himself up as he wailed in pain and surprise. I held the two of them there for long enough to have a good cry and then collect myself. I explained to Noah why I'd done it. He was incredulous. To my knowledge Jacob never knew what hit him or how he fell. I'd like to say that as we sat on the sidewalk, a car going too fast whizzed out of the driveway or through the cross street, vindicating my actions, but that didn't occur. Jacob's hands were grazed and bleeding. His jeans were torn, revealing knees that were bleeding, as well.

We gathered ourselves together, Noah suggesting that we all hold hands and Jacob complying, for once, and made it into the flat without another incident. Of course, Jacob had to jump up both flights of stairs, annoying the retired, single woman in the ground floor flat. He kicked off his shoes against the door before jumping the length of the flat to his toys. I shut myself in the bathroom and had another long cry.

I'm crying now. I knew that if I was able to stop him with my handbag that I would hurt him. I knew it wouldn't hurt him badly, not anything like getting hit by a car would hurt him. It never crossed my mind how much it would hurt me.

The Sky Is the Limit

Everybody has occasional bad days that seem to go on forever, when nothing seems to go right. But we were having a lot of them. And for the most part, they seemed unavoidable. I mean, what do you do when your 4-year-old is terrified of water but definitely needs a bath? What if every time you try to bathe him, he literally fights for his life, as if he believes he's dying? And we're talking really, literally, thinks he's dying, as in fight-for-your-life-someone-is-trying-to-drown-you dying.

It didn't matter whether it was 2 inches of water in the tub, or 10. For 2 years, our son, Greg, suffered debilitating panic attacks every time he was bathed. Just the thought of bathing him was exhausting and required a determined effort; I had to work myself up to it. Bathing Greg could not be done in a few minutes before bed. I had to prepare for it. I would get the bath water ready, preferably while he was outside or in another part of the house so he wouldn't hear it, change into something I didn't mind getting soaked, and then go to get him ready.

Everything was fine until Greg realized what was about to happen, and then even getting him undressed was a challenge. Once he was undressed, I would attempt to lift him into the tub, but it was like wrestling an octopus: Even though he only had four limbs, he fought so hard it seemed like eight. His arms would hold on for dear life in a stranglehold around my neck. His legs would do anything they could to avoid touching water. And when they finally did, they didn't stay in it for long. Greg would kick and thrash and try to climb the side of the tub. It was easier once I got him into a seated position because he would then lose the leverage of his legs. But it still was challenging. It took all my strength to hold him in the water and try to wash him.

There was so much kicking, flailing, and screaming. It was chaos. The worst part for me was washing Greg's hair. Trying to tip his head back to rinse out the soap I had scrubbed into his hair with a washcloth made me feel as if I were trying to drown my own child. I was right there, face to face with him. So close. So intimate. And I could see the absolute terror in his eyes. No mother ever wants to be the cause of her baby's terror. It was so disheartening. So emotionally draining. So completely heartbreaking.

By the end of his bath, when he was finally released, Greg would run away, wrapped in his towel, with his head covered as if in a tent, and he would curl up in a ball and hide. We had to let him decompress for a few minutes before we could dry him off and dress him. Who am I kidding? I needed to decompress too, to catch my breath. I felt bad in every way possible. I was exhausted after the workout, and felt like the worst parent on the planet.

Afterward Greg would be really quiet, and look at me with suspicion—as if he wondered why I would do such a terrible thing to him and what I was going to do to him next. It broke my heart every time we had to bathe him. Showers were just as bad. Greg couldn't even handle being sprinkled and would have a meltdown if we were caught out in the rain. And yet he had to be cleaned. That, for me, was the worst moment of our autism journey so far.

If we had lived in an apartment, I'm sure we would have been reported for child abuse. The noise was incredible. But to us, it had become "normal," just as anything you go through on a repeated basis becomes normal. I remember realizing how bad things were when my dad came to visit. After witnessing one bathing experience, he shook his head sadly, and asked quietly, "Is it like that every time you give him a bath?" At that moment I realized that, yes, this really was pretty bad.

We tried to limit the frequency of his baths, but you only can avoid bathing a 4-year-old boy only for so long. Even washing Greg's hands was a challenge. We had to forcefully hold his hands under the faucet. Soap was completely out of the question; he couldn't handle the slimy texture. And if we did manage to sneak soap onto his hands, it was all we could do to hold him in place long enough to rinse it off. The more Greg fought us, the stronger he got, and the more difficult each session became.

To make matters worse, it wasn't just the bathing that set him off. Going to a doctor's office, even if he wasn't the one being seen, would trigger a similar response. So did several other things at home. We learned to avoid triggering Greg. We taught our other children to be sensitive to the things that made him upset and to avoid doing them. We learned how to tell when he was starting to get worked up and did everything we could to avert a meltdown. But it wasn't always avoidable. And once the meltdown began, it was impossible to stop. There was nothing we could do aside from riding out the storm.

So maybe that was more than a "worst moment." It was more like a "worst season." Thankfully, we're not there anymore. In fact, it is hard to believe the difference between the child we have today and the child he was 3 years ago. At our latest evaluation meeting just this month, the administrator told us she had never seen so much improvement in any child—especially not in such a short time.

So what changed? Greg had lots of intensive therapy. He participated in horseback riding therapy through a local nonprofit. He had the typical run of occupational, physical, and speech therapy sessions, and we enrolled him in school, even though we had intended to homeschool him. We have been a homeschooling family for almost 20 years, and it was a difficult decision to make. But the difference in the frequency of therapy the school was offering if we homeschooled versus sending him to school was staggering, so we swallowed our pride and sent him to school. But it turned out to be the best thing for him. We plan to evaluate as we go along, but so far it has been a very positive experience, and the kids have all accepted him and seem to like him.

The one change we believe has had the most positive impact, especially on bath time, is swim therapy. Greg goes to the pool twice a week, working with an instructor one-on-one in the water for 30- to 45-minute sessions. When he first started water therapy 1½ years ago, Greg had a panic attack just walking through the doors to the pool. He had another meltdown when he was forced to dip his toe into the water. But over time, they encouraged him to do more. He slowly learned to push himself to do things that were scary or outside his comfort zone. Step one, foot in. Splash his instructor. Splash his own belly. Sit in the water. Our pool has a gradual entry. It's like walking into the water at a beach, rather than stairs that step down into the water; it is only 1 or 2 inches deeper with each step. Now he loves the water. He's very proud of himself for being able to doggy paddle around the current channel.

He can't really swim yet—he's still too stiff for that—but he's making good progress. He even stiffly floats on his back while his instructor supports him. Greg is not quite relaxed enough to float, but he's very proud of himself for not being afraid. For the longest time, he wouldn't put his face in the water—not his ears, mouth, or nose. Now he can dip his ears in without much trouble. He will tentatively blow bubbles now and dip his nose in just a bit. He has been under water completely a few times, although he doesn't really like it. But it is such great progress from where he was.

Just a couple of weeks ago, Greg was in his first school program. I cried through the whole thing. The program was "The Little Engine That Could Sing." He was the back half of the Rusty Crusty Train Engine, and he performed flawlessly. He followed the boy who was the front half of the engine and went where he was supposed to go. After his part was over, he climbed up on the risers with the other children and stood still, just as he was supposed to do. He wasn't afraid of the crowd. The lights didn't bother him. And even though Greg still has issues when people sing, the music at the program didn't bother him. He didn't sing, but he also didn't cover his ears and drop to the floor the way he used to do. Three years ago, he would have had a panic-attack-style meltdown over any one of those things. But there he was, actually enjoying being in the play. We had held him out of the kindergarten play because we didn't think there was any way he would be able to handle it. Yet here he was, a year later, performing like a pro. He even seemed less nervous than at least a quarter of the other students.

So I guess the biggest lesson I've learned through all of this is not to assume that where we are today is where we will always be. There is a tendency to expect the worst when your child is diagnosed with autism. I remember wondering if we dared hope that Greg eventually would be able to live on his own as an adult. Now I am confident that he will. Not only will he survive, he will thrive. I'm encouraged by the huge leap he has made in the past few years and am cautiously optimistic that he might find a niche where he not only will do well, but also will excel. We've still got a long road ahead of us, but we're going to be fine. The sky is the limit for this kid, just as it is for any other child. I can't wait to see who he becomes!

Splashes of Color

"I can't believe he just said that!" remarked my youngest brother, Paul, a few years ago. My brother's startled comment was a response to a jaw-dropping statement made by our son, Matthew. Paul's surprise was perfectly understandable; Matthew's random, unexpected comments often startle people who are not well acquainted with him. Almost without fail, if Matthew wants to say something, he says it! The same is true of his actions: If Matthew wants to do something, he does it!

Speaking and acting impulsively with little regard for potential consequences is not unusual for 21-year-olds. But Matthew's diminished forethought goes beyond that, occurring much more frequently than for other young adults. Moreover, he does not readily learn from his mistakes. He needs a lot of repetition and support; even then, his success rate is spotty.

You see, our very likable, funny, impulsive son was diagnosed with autism during his third-grade school year. Impulsivity has been a major manifestation of Matthew's autism throughout his life. Even today, low impulse control has had a huge impact on practically every part of his life. He has trouble making and keeping friends. Similarly, he has trouble getting jobs and keeping them. Matthew's behaviors affect everyone around him, whether they are close family members or strangers whom he encounters in a restaurant. At home and in public, his unpredictable words and actions range from being downright hilarious to horrifyingly embarrassing; pull-your-hair-out-frustrating to monetarily expensive; and offensively gross to potentially dangerous.

Compared with many other individuals with autism, Matthew is fairly extroverted, and he often tries engaging others in conversation— whether he knows them or not. Yet autism hinders his ability to read the body language and facial expressions of other people. Matthew often misses the mark in gauging his behaviors accordingly. For instance, he might keep talking about his favorite rock bands long past the point of most people's active interest in the conversation. Taking this limitation to a higher level, Matthew has made untimely, sexual remarks at his previous place of employment: a senior care facility.

Recently, Matthew and my husband, Jason, attended our local caucus for the upcoming presidential election. Matthew and Jason were supporting different candidates, so they sat at different tables. Without hesitation or preventive restraint from his dad, Matthew volunteered to run as a delegate to represent his favored political candidate at the county caucus. Upon volunteering, Matthew gave a brief, impromptu speech, explaining his reasons for supporting that particular candidate and why he should be considered as a delegate representative. To the surprise of my husband, and later to me, Matthew was elected to be one of the three county delegates for that candidate! Matthew's fearlessness never ceases to amaze us.

Matthew's desire to connect with others, however, at times has put him in potentially dangerous situations. For example, he has approached strangers with the intention of complimenting their tattoos and body piercings. Although some welcome Matthew's friendly overtures, others react negatively, almost to the point of hostility. On more than one occasion, people have needed to physically intervene to save Matthew from getting his face punched in.

I suppose we have all been guilty of seeing or hearing things the way we want to, regardless of whether our perceptions correspond to actual reality. Yet for Matthew, this phenomenon occurs regularly, sometimes with costly consequences.

Music of almost every style and genre (except "country") is Matthew's number one passion, so getting new music to listen to is a treat. His dad offered to buy him one or two albums per month, provided that Matthew's overall behavior warranted the purchases. By the way, Matthew likes to have entire collections of particular artists. Because Matthew heard his dad's "promise" of music acquisition through his own filter, coupled with his impulsivity, he decided to grasp the opportunity himself.

At that time, iTunes did not require logging in with a password before making a purchase. Therefore, when Matthew went to the family computer, he was able to download albums by the thrash metal band, Slayer. Not just one or two of Slayer's albums, but the entire collection—roughly $300 worth! He clicked the "Purchase" key, one album after the other, until he had downloaded everything available Slayer had ever recorded.

Fortunately, when this episode occurred, Jason received e-mail notification from Apple informing him that $300 worth of purchases had just been made from his account. Taking quick action, Jason called Apple and persuaded the company to void the $300 charge on our account.

Shortly after that, Jason issued our son a strong reprimand, explaining to Matthew why his impulsive actions could have been costly for our family. He also warned Matthew *never* to make any kind of electronic purchase without having first received his dad's approval. Given the sternness of the reprimand, one might expect that Matthew would exercise more thought before repeating his behavior in that sort of situation again. As we would soon learn, the message apparently did not completely sink in.

Not long after the Apple event, Matthew decided that he wanted some *Jackass* movies from Amazon and proceeded to purchase $100 worth of movies. From his standpoint, having a slew of *Jackass* was true delight. However, this once again demonstrated his inability to generalize life lessons.

After this second event, Jason's patience with our son was wearing thin. So, once again, he explained to Matthew why he must leave all electronics purchases to his father. I wish I could say Matthew had learned his lesson and was successful in restraining his impulsive purchases without prior approval from his parents. In short order, Matthew took his father's Kindle and proceeded to buy without permission. Strike three.

Because of Matthew's ongoing difficulty with impulse restraint, we now frequently remind him, "Matthew, you must ask for our permission before [fill in the blank]. And you must wait until we say 'yes' to your request. Otherwise you do *not* have permission to do what you want."

If we're trying to identify the "worst" moment for our family, it could be measured in dollars, or from the sinking realization that

Matthew will go to any length to gratify his wishes. We also realized that teaching Matthew to consider the consequences of his behaviors in advance would take much more effort on everyone's part and also would take longer than we had anticipated.

In hindsight, I wish Jason and I had exercised more consistency in our attempts to teach Matthew the importance of practicing self-control. I don't know if we would have been successful. All we know is that we are called to be faithful in teaching our son in the very best way we can.

Indeed, Matthew's unpredictable behaviors have created additional challenges for every member of our family—Jason and me, as well as for his sisters. Nevertheless, we truly thank the Lord for giving us the honor of having Matthew in our family. Countless times, I've told Matthew that I couldn't possibly love another son as much as I love him. Therefore, as we pause a moment to consider this endearing young man, we are grateful for the unexpected splashes of color he brings to this world. And we look forward to his bringing us more surprises tomorrow.

Summary

In an ideal world, we wouldn't have this chapter, but that would ignore the genuine experience of being a parent of children on the autism spectrum. If you have more than one child, there is the constant worry about the impact of ASD on the other sibling(s). For some parents, the primary worry is the impact of one child on the other. But from a considerably more vulnerable standpoint, stories within this chapter expose the impact of seeing our own parenting choices reflected in the eyes of our children. Sometimes, it is the look we see in our loved one's eyes that allows us to acknowledge the reality of our situation.

As parents, a balance must be achieved between acknowledging the emotional impact and engaging in the practical problem solving. Every day, parents raising children on the spectrum are wrestling with questions such as, "How do you bathe a 4-year-old?" and "How do you prevent your young adult from bankrupting you?"

We have not added a list of resources to this chapter. Each parenting moment is unique and challenging in its own way. These moments are too emotional to distill into a bullet point, so we won't. All parents process these challenging emotional moments in their own way. At the risk of adding one more task to the long list of parenting duties, we politely request that you make time for yourself: Connect, play, and create, so you can be the parent you are meant to be.

five

"Picking the locks to open the doors of the world for exceptional children": The Poignant Moments of Raising a Child With ASD

As it turns out, your child can teach *you* as much as you teach your child. Certainly, you will teach your child how to navigate social norms, read faces, and develop organizational skills. Meanwhile, your child will teach you about the meaning of life—the beauty of patterns and seeing life through a different lens. Some of those lessons may come in the form of a monologue, which must not be interrupted. Parents were asked to describe the poignant lessons they have learned along the way, intentionally or not, and to share the insights they gained.

Locksmith Needed!

Meet Ava, 8 years old. Obsessed with Minecraft, Teenage Mutant Ninja Turtles, horses, and cats of all sizes. Cannot get enough of swings, trampolines, PJs, stuffed animals, and milk chocolate. Can melt your heart with an out-of-the-blue bear hug and a crooked, teeth-too-big-for-her-mouth smile—just as quickly as she can out-ninja most of the neighborhood boys her age with her toy sword and nunchuck collection! Hurtling herself into life at 100 miles per hour, she is a 40-pound, fierce and determined pixie who follows her passions without hesitation or second thought.

Pretty typical scrappy 8-year-old, right?

Ava also has some rather exceptional qualities. She can, for example, watch a movie one time and, upon hearing the soundtrack weeks or even months later, describe in detail exactly what scenes were taking place during every musical score, including instrumental ones.

Ava also can process higher-level concepts that one would not expect a young child to understand. She often quietly absorbs information and will then shock us by applying that concept to a completely different subject months later. She is especially drawn to songs, story morals, and religious meanings.

She recently finished watching the movie *Dennis the Menace* for the first time. She suddenly ran through the house, calling for me in an urgent voice: "Mom! Mom! I completely understand now!"

"What do you understand?" I asked.

"I just finished the movie, and now I understand! 'The one who tries to trick a wise one, only fools himself'!"

Whoa. The only meaning I personally got out of that movie was that a flaming marshmallow can inflict a lot of pain after flying through the air and getting stuck to your forehead. (Mr. Wilson, you poor man!)

In sharing this story with her teacher a few days later, I learned that this moral briefly had been mentioned as part of an animal story they had read months earlier.

We are finding that Ava's brain categorizes amazing amounts of information, but to gain access to this information requires a very specific method or process. Ask her questions, and she will likely stare blankly back at you for several minutes and potentially never reply. Ask her the same questions while she is sitting on a moving swing, and she will reply easily and fluidly. It is much like picking the lock of a booby-trapped safe: Enter the combination incorrectly, and she will likely blow up into a frustrated tantrum. Enter the combination correctly, and you could be presented with the meaning of life!

Ava might now be sounding a bit more complicated than a run-of-the-mill, typical 8-year old, yes? Now add in her incredibly high levels of ADHD symptoms, frequent inability to make eye contact, difficulty reading social cues, preference to play in-parallel versus interacting with peers, and total confusion with sarcasm, double meanings, or jokes. Consider her inability to understand when to speak in a quiet voice (Church services are always eventful!), her sensory challenges, and her love of all things VELCRO® ... and now we are venturing even further from most people's definition of "neurotypical."

Ava's behaviors first began to concern us as she progressed from toddler to preschool years. She became less age-appropriate and more puzzling. While she could speak, her verbal skills were delayed. She was not sleeping well. She tested with perfect hearing, yet seldom reacted when we called her name. She was not interested in other children. She acted as if they were invisible, literally stepping on top of them or colliding with them while she played alone.

"Ava, please do not step on other children. Ava. Ava? Ava? AVA!?"

Don't even get me started about play dates and birthday parties. Or lack thereof.

Ava struggled in her early school years. Parent–teacher conferences all had the same theme: "Perhaps your daughter would be more successful at a special school where she could get more services and accommodations or have smaller class sizes?"

Ava changed schools four times before she entered second grade.

From the extensive amount of research I consumed (in place of that pesky human need to sleep), I came to the conclusion that Ava likely was on the autism spectrum. She was receiving occupational therapy from the age of 2, and we were seeing only minimal results. ABA (applied behavioral analysis) therapy sounded like a much better fit for her. Unfortunately, insurance would not cover the high cost of ABA therapy without an autism diagnosis.

I launched a quest to help my daughter. Ava was formally evaluated on four separate occasions at private clinics, costing thousands of dollars. Finally, at 8 years old and from her fourth evaluation, she received an autism diagnosis. I had learned two valuable lessons: Be persistent, and trust my gut. I implore all parents who go through any similar process with their children: Trust your instincts! I second-guessed myself several times over the 5 years between Ava's first to last evaluation, and it led to delays that may have had a negative impact on my child.

Why the misdiagnoses?

In my opinion, there are two primary reasons: The first is that Ava is female, and the second is that she presents with several comorbid conditions, which may have overshadowed her symptoms of autism.

According to the Centers for Disease Control (cdc.gov/ncbddd/autism/facts.html), boys are nearly five times more likely than girls to have autism. Does this fact sometimes skew evaluations? In our experience, I would give this a resounding YES. It makes sense that females may present with different ASD symptoms than males. Perhaps even their similar symptoms are interpreted differently because of gender profiling.

Ava was first evaluated at a clinic specializing in sensory processing disorder (SPD). The developmental pediatrician assured me that Ava absolutely did not have ADHD or autism, but only sensory processing disorder. I was told that the majority of children at that clinic who are diagnosed with ADHD and/or autism are males, and I should not be concerned.

"Ava is so social—look how she is smiling and following directions! She is very charming! This is not ADHD or autism." The doctor left the room without any further discussion. Case closed. I was left feeling like a web-trolling idiot with Munchausen syndrome by proxy.

This doctor and therapy team evaluated her on two occasions within 2 years because her symptoms not only were continuing, but becoming more problematic. The same diagnosis was given, and my concerns were dismissed. Years of early intervention therapy missed.

People with autism also are likely to have comorbid conditions. These can include disorders of the gastrointestinal system, visual problems, seizure disorders, ADHD, Tourette syndrome, intellectual disabilities, a host of neuropsychological disorders, and more.

During a comprehensive evaluation at age 6, Ava was exhibiting several of her autism symptoms. Unfortunately, she also was exhibiting many behaviors associated with her comorbid ADHD disorder. She had become so dysregulated that she simply sat on the floor, laughing and spinning in circles. Was this ADHD or autism? The evaluating doctors and therapists chose ADHD.

In the course of that evaluation, Ava was able to converse with adults when prompted, occasionally make eye contact, and follow directions. (Her social challenges are much worse with peers than with adults.) She entertained and charmed the adult team (while repetitively lining up all of her toys and quoting lines from *The Lion King* movie). All of this added up to a negated autism diagnosis.

"She is smart-as-a-whip and too cute to be on the autism spectrum! She simply needs to slow down," the developmental pediatrician relayed with a kind, yet dismissive, smile.

We had waited 8 months for this evaluation appointment, only to hit a brick wall once again.

We were advised to continue occupational therapy and to consider ADHD medications. Instead of feeling relieved that Ava had a diagnosis, I felt like crying. Would the doctors feel the same way about her behaviors if they had watched her at school, laughing through the day without focusing or learning? Would they tell her teachers to view her disruptive stimming (using repetitive sounds and movements to help reduce anxiety and self-soothe) and lack of social skills as "cute?" How "cute" would these behaviors look when she was 13 years old? Or 18? Or 25?

I wanted a diagnosis that would help my child receive accommodations at school! Therapy that would actually make a difference in her behavior! I desperately needed to find help for my daughter, so her future would be less challenging and more successful. After 2 years of treading water and me looking things up, things were no better at home. Ava was now 8 years old. Her daily life was filled with challenges that led to constant frustrated tantrums; we still lacked guidance and an accurate diagnosis.

I continued researching autism, and I attended a conference featuring Dr. Temple Grandin and Dr. Raun Melmed as key speakers. What I had not anticipated was that this day would mark a turning point in my life. I listened to both speakers discuss autistic behaviors and how to help children manage and find success at school and home. I listened as they described my daughter! Our family!

Dr. Melmed began the day by addressing the evaluation process. He spoke of his respect for the opinions of parents with whom he works. Parents know their children much better than a doctor who spends a few hours with the child in an evaluation environment. Who is he to tell them that they are wrong after just a short initial glimpse? He urged the attending professionals not to dismiss concerned parents but to respect and include them as an important diagnostic piece of their child's puzzle. I grabbed a tissue. It would not be the only one that day.

I left that conference feeling that my concerns were validated. I was fired up! No giving up, no more being shushed by uninformed professionals! Immediately upon leaving the conference, I researched and found another highly regarded assessment clinic.

Six months later, Ava was evaluated yet again, and finally we felt that she received complete and accurate diagnoses.

Ava has now been diagnosed with high-functioning autism. Her comorbid diagnoses include severe ADHD, developmental coordination disorder, sensory processing disorder, and migraine headaches that present as Alice-in-Wonderland syndrome (causing visual and auditory hallucinations). She also struggles with food allergies, gastrointestinal intolerances, and sleep and visual disorders.

After her diagnosis, Ava qualified for ABA therapy. She began receiving 13 hours of ABA therapy both at school and at home every week. Within just 6 months of beginning this protocol, her behaviors markedly improved. Her teachers were astounded by her social skill growth at school, and her grades were excellent! The less-structured hours at home were slower to improve but also transforming. Committing to helping our child also meant committing to modifying our parenting methods and lifestyles to provide a constant therapy protocol. It was with great relief that we finally began seeing dramatic reductions in her frustration levels (and ours).

While we understand that Ava will carry these diagnoses throughout her life, we also understand that the earlier a child receives intervention, the better her prognosis. I felt as if I were racing against a ticking clock for years. It is commonly understood that the brain is most responsive to interventions before age 5, but Ava was not diagnosed until she was 8. As we started our journey, we already were behind schedule. On the one hand, I know many girls are not diagnosed until their teenage years, so I feel fortunate that we found answers as early as we did. On the other hand, ticktock . . .

Life's journey as a special-needs parent is a lesson in humility and perseverance. I have learned to listen to my inner voice and to trust myself. I have learned that no matter how many initials follow a person's name—MD, PhD, OTR/L, LCSW, and so on—they do not spell GOD.

My role as the special-needs parent is to locate the best professionals to help my child, to compile all the information and opinions from all different specialties involved, and to determine the course of action myself. It is important to keep an open mind, to be willing to admit and move on from your mistakes, and to never give up on yourself or your child. I have learned to appreciate the knowledge and skill set of each professional we have hired, but I also understand that each one has a limited focus and brings only one piece to the puzzle that is my job to complete.

As overwhelming as this journey can get at times, life has a way of providing me with little gifts that fuel the fire within my heart, to keep me forging ahead. A gift might be a positive report from a teacher, hearing a child call, "Hi Ava!" upon a chance meeting at the supermarket, or suddenly noticing that I have not seen my child rocking on the floor or chewing VELCRO® in the past week!

The greatest gifts, however, come from my child. Watching Ava exude joy and exuberance toward her passions in life while dealing with daily struggles that I cannot imagine, is humbling. I take for granted how easy it is to simply eat, dress myself, and jot down notes on my calendar. My child has feeding difficulties and seldom can find a sock that does not inspire screaming. Her handwriting is almost illegible, on a good day. These things don't stop her. She powers through and often finds shortcuts to help herself.

Ava once was described by a friend as "hurtling herself at life." This is exactly what she does. She throws herself 110% into everything she feels strongly about, whether it's the music she loves, a subject she is interested in, her schoolwork, or a person for whom she cares.

If her actions are not quite fitting into society's norms, it does not stop her. That she cares little about others' judgment often results in people being drawn to her—quite the opposite of what I had, in her earlier years, expected. In her special, black-and-white thinking, she simply cannot understand why people would not always be honest and true to themselves and to others.

She teaches me that life is about living and not holding anything back. It may be an autistic quality, but it is one of her best—and one I try to emulate. One of Ava's favorite thoughts to share is this: "The most important thing in life is LIFE. Without it, we wouldn't be anything." I wonder if she understands the weight of truth in those simple words.

We must persist in picking the locks to open the doors of the world for such exceptional children as Ava, because they just might have the power to transform it. Calling all locksmiths . . .

Resources
Centers for Disease Control and Prevention (2016). Facts about ASD. Retrieved from www.cdc.gov/ncbddd/autism/facts.html
The Melmed Center (Dr. Raun Melmed). Retrieved from melmedcenter. com
Temple Grandin, PhD. Retrieved from templegrandin.com

Looking Back and Remembering Moments With Gordon

As a parent of a child with autism there are moments I remember and some I'd like to forget. Our daughter was born with an extra toe that required surgical correction, so at the first moment our son, Gordon, was born, I looked at his feet. Only 10 toes! Yay! I said to my husband, "You wait; there'll probably be something wrong that we can't see." Almost 4 years later, our son would be diagnosed with pervasive developmental disorder (PDD). Whew, not autism, what a relief! The autism diagnosis came later and was one of the best things that happened, primarily because more people had heard of autism.

When Gordon was born I remember being so happy to have a son who would someday carry on the family name. I can't remember now, but I probably had names picked out for my future grandchildren. A couple of decades later I wonder why that was even important to me. Will Gordon marry and have children? I have no idea. Thoughts of grandchildren are one of the last things on my mind now. Gordon has taught me to pay attention to the present rather than dwell on the past or worry about the future.

Speaking of grandchildren, Gordon is one of six on my side of the family, one of three on the other side. One of my favorite memories from long ago is my father telling me about a tantrum that 3-year-old Gordon threw in a convenience store. How was Grampa to know that Gordon wanted a bag of his favorite rainbow-colored candy? Thanks to a lot of hard work, Gordon and Grampa can communicate just fine, and every once in a while, we say, "Remember when he couldn't tell us which candy he wanted?" Now he's able to let us know which specific variety of the favorite rainbow-colored candy he wants!

Gordon was a difficult infant. By difficult I mean he cried constantly, hated breastfeeding, didn't tolerate regular formula, and barely accepted soy formula. We were living in a German-speaking country at the time; I was able to speak German well enough to communicate with his pediatrician, who assured me that constant crying wasn't typical, but that it was normal. I accepted that explanation, and, somehow, we all made it through his first year. As a side note, I ask you to imagine a screaming 6-month-old Gordon being babysat by the German-speaking child-minders at a fitness club I had joined (and I am not ashamed to admit that I traded the pain of working out in exchange for having someone else watch Gordon and his sister for an hour each day). I should have realized it was odd that he was the only child who wouldn't settle, the only child who wouldn't play with others, the only child who had to be walked and bounced for the entire hour by a cigarette-smoking cleaning lady who had been drafted by the child-minders because she was the only one who could tolerate Gordon for any length of time. No wonder she would come find me at the end of the hour: She had to get back to work!

Gordon's speech developed at a typical pace for his first 2 years. We went to play groups. We visited friends (despite his behavior often being described as "terrible" by those same friends). I'm sure he talked. I have a photo of Gordon holding a plastic telephone and pretending to call his dad. He's even smiling in the photo! It was only after we made the transatlantic move back to the United States that I realized he was not only stagnant with his speech growth, but he also seemed to be losing words, as well. Gordon's pediatrician assured me it was just because his older sister talked for him. I didn't believe that, because it wasn't accurate; I assumed he was having trouble understanding the people around him because he was hearing English instead of German. I was right about his sister not talking for him. I was wrong about the English-German confusion. When I finally convinced the HMO pediatrician that perhaps Gordon needed to be seen by a speech therapist, I was able to get him an hour of speech therapy per week. I, of course, in the remaining hours each week, was to make every effort to engage him in conversation. Did the speech therapist think I had been giving him the silent treatment? At no point did the speech therapist mention autism, although the report is full of comments I now recognize as red flags. We have all learned a lot about autism since 1994.

When Gordon started preschool I met the first in a long line of paraprofessionals who were crucial to his success in school. In the course of our initial conversation, this particular paraprofessional told me that her 16-year-old daughter with Rett syndrome was nonverbal. What was my response? "Wow." At the time I had never heard the term, "nonverbal," and I certainly didn't apply it to Gordon. In retrospect, Gordon was nearly nonverbal at the time. He also had significant behavioral issues. He kicked, he hit, he ran away, he refused to follow directions, and he tried to bite. Somehow, I didn't realize Gordon's behaviors were not typical of a 3-year-old. I may have been in denial, but Gordon's pediatricians assured me that he was doing fine … just a little speech delay. And I wanted to believe them.

We owe so much to this amazing paraprofessional who knew enough about autism and who cared enough about Gordon to tell me that he likely would benefit from more intensive services. She was right. She encouraged and inspired me to advocate for Gordon when I was more than willing to ignore everything and just settle for a little calmness in my life while he was at preschool. We appreciate her more than she will ever know. Not only did she make a huge difference for

Gordon, she inspired me to become involved in special education so I could make a difference for someone else's child.

My husband traveled extensively for business while Gordon and his sister were growing up. Finding a sitter who was willing to stay with Gordon was next to impossible. If I wanted to go anywhere, I brought the kids with me. I wanted to be as involved as possible in community activities and had an opportunity to host someone who was traveling the country with the international singing and dancing troupe Up With People. What a great idea! The kids and I attended the packed meeting at the cafeteria in the local middle school. Gordon and I stood as far in the back as we could, so that his displeasure at not being allowed to run around would impact the fewest people. He squirmed and protested. I'm sure we looked like a picture of sweaty distress while I tried to keep him contained and quiet during the presentation. I thought I had it under control until a pleasant-looking woman approached me. Naive me, I thought she was going to offer words of encouragement or solace. Nope. She curtly asked me to keep Gordon quiet because she couldn't hear the presentation. I'm afraid my stress-induced response was something like, "Then move closer if you can't hear! I can't get any farther away!" I hope the sweat on my face masked the tears leaking from my eyes. Couldn't she see I was trying?

There were many incidents like the one in the middle school cafeteria. Shopping was a nightmare. The looks clearly communicated: "What's wrong with that kid?" "Why is he harnessed to the shopping cart? Can't she see he just wants to get out of the seat?" Most of the time I kept my head down and shopped as quickly as possible, or shopped when Gordon was at preschool—such a relief! There was one particularly noisy incident in a bookstore when we were visiting my parents. I can't remember how it started, but Gordon decided to throw himself on the floor and scream at the top of his lungs. I don't remember how I reacted. I do remember my acute embarrassment when an elderly gentleman had to step around us. Then it happened; he made eye contact with me. My defenses sprang up, and then he said, "You're doing the right thing." Ahhh ... thank you.

Just for fun, my husband and I attended a psychic fair. Gordon was 3 at the time and used few words. A psychic told us that one day

Gordon would address a large group of people. Right. Gordon the pretty much nonverbal child will make a speech. That statement stuck with me, though. As it turns out, Gordon *has* addressed groups of people. He spoke about his high school work experiences to a group of visitors from Asia who were collaborating with a local university to find ways to help their population with autism. Every time he visits his grandparents in New England, he attends "senior church" with them and never fails to greet every single person he sees. "Good morning, I'm Gordon. How are you?" The church members are primarily senior citizens. This young man who makes it a priority to spend time with them charms most of them. Only one person described Gordon's manner as "overbearing" and wondered why he insisted on greeting the parishioners each time he saw them. I felt hurt and offended when I heard about the comment, but Gordon's grandparents took it in stride and reminded the church member that Gordon worked very hard to gain his speech and social skills, and they were proud of him for reaching out. I'm proud of him, too.

We've always loved Gordon. We have not always understood or enjoyed his actions. Thinking back over our lives together to compile these poignant moments has given me a chance to reflect on the remarkable young man he has become. The toddler whose behavior was described as "terrible" is now a gentleman who offers to help in any way he can. The elementary school student who was a very picky eater now cooks his own meals and packs well-balanced lunches to bring to work every day. The middle school student who wanted to wear sandals every single day now chooses a variety of footwear according to the weather and the occasion (He has been known to bring along spare shoes, just in case!). The high school student who was given the opportunity to engage in work experiences inside and outside of the school building now works 20 hours per week in paid employment. The child who required our undivided attention and instruction now gives *us* advice on how to have a calm and peaceful day. The boy who was "born with only 10 toes and probably something else wrong with him" still has 10 toes, and I now know that there is nothing wrong with him at all. There never was. He has autism. He's Gordon. We can't wait to see what the future holds.

Better Than Anyone ...

Trying to determine my most poignant lesson of raising a son who is on the autism spectrum is like trying to count the stars. It is an impossible task, and if I begin to try, I lose count and begin to focus on the ones with which I am most familiar. My son, Josh, has changed who I am, the way I think, the way I see the world, and the way I interact with others. I have wrestled with the concept of "one thing" to share with you, and I have come away with only this: Help others to know the child you know better than anyone.

Having a child with Asperger's is a special blessing, although there are moments, if we are perfectly honest with ourselves, when it seems more like a curse. I want to encourage you to always remember, even though there will be struggles that you could never have imagined, you have an extremely important role in this extremely important person's life. I remember sobbing and crying out loud because I didn't (and still don't) have the answers I needed to be a better parent for my son. My faith played a huge role in keeping me sane. I always have known that God has great plans for Josh, and it's not important that I know the "why" right now. You *will* get through it, but it probably won't be easy or quick. Realize that there are times when you will be completely overwhelmed and frustrated. Hang on ... it will get better.

Sometimes we don't need advice; we just need someone to listen. At other times, we don't have anything to say; we just need someone to tell us what to do. Surrounding yourself whenever possible with people who can understand what you are going through and offer advice when needed can reduce an insurmountable challenge into a minor upset. There were times when Josh was younger that I could have used the social support of friends and families sharing similar experiences of raising a child on the spectrum. Both of my parents passed away before I realized my son had Asperger's, and even then, the diagnosis was a very new thing. I often wondered, "Is this normal behavior?" So in the effort to try to figure things out on my own, I often became a "mama grizzly." I always have been maximally protective of Josh if I felt there was a threat. Because I lacked a sounding board, I constantly struggled internally with the question: *Why did they see my son differently than I saw him?*

Life is hard. There is no getting around that. It may sometimes seem unfair. But our attitude can be the difference in how we help our children grow in a world that wants to box them in. The world always will judge your child's external features and behaviors. You cannot control the world, and you cannot isolate your child from the cruelty he or she will face, no matter how hard you try. It has been my experience, no matter what age my son has been, that some people are just plain mean. Whether deliberate or not, the end result is the same: pain, tears, and, hopefully, lessons learned. You can prepare and support your child when challenges arise. Be your child's number one advocate, no matter what. This does not mean allowing him to do things that are wrong or inappropriate. It means that when you see injustice being done to your child, you need to have his back; in the process, you can help other people to better know and love the child you know better than anyone.

When Josh was in second grade, my husband and I went to the school for his regular IEP (individualized education program). At one point during the meeting, my son's teacher stood up and began making fun of his walk. She even laughed as she did it. I was stunned (and more than a little angry), and as I looked around the room, I believe she had the same effect on the other education professionals. I made it clear that unless her comments could benefit the situation, I wasn't interested in her impersonation. As I look back on this incident, it still saddens me that someone in a role of influence in Josh's life would reduce his behavior to a joke. I'm sure it was not ill-intended; most insensitive comments or actions are simply a matter of the person not being aware of how they are perceived. I don't hold it against her, but I am glad I spoke out. She was then able to see a little better the child I knew better than anyone.

When Josh got a little older, it became more evident that the people who were designated to help him were not sufficiently educated on how to deal with a child on the spectrum. I tried to work as closely as I could with them, suggesting creative ways they could avoid disruptions or misbehavior in the classroom and how to help him excel. But no matter what I did, they still put him into a metaphorical box they didn't really want to open.

I began to have discussions with a woman who worked at a private school, and over the course of a few months she became an advocate for Josh and me. She not only wanted to be my son's teacher, she also went out of her way to help develop a way that *all* of the teachers and administrators within her school would learn how to effectively teach children on the autism spectrum. When Josh started sixth grade at her school the next fall, he was welcomed with open arms, and he felt more valued there than he had in his entire academic career. For example, if Josh said or did something unusual, the teachers helped the other students understand, and taught them how to respond in ways that would benefit everyone. I will forever be grateful to that teacher for seeing the child whom I thought only I understood.

I grew up in a home where both of my parents worked in public education, and doing well in school was highly regarded. I still hold strong to this value, but it has changed since having a son with Asperger's. Certain things always have been easy for my son, academics and music being two of his major strengths. Josh has an incredible photographic memory, and I don't think he ever has spelled a word wrong in his life. However, while I applauded son's brilliance in his ability to recite all of the state capitals by the time he was 3, I overlooked what seems so basic that most people take it for granted: *the fundamental need to be socially accepted.*

Many individuals with Asperger's have something they do that only can be described as "incredible." Maybe they are a math wiz or a prodigy artist, or they understand animal behavior unlike anyone has ever seen. Josh has an outstanding musical ability. It doesn't come from anything anyone on Earth has taught him. This is something that comes naturally to him. Throughout his life, Josh has received accolades for his musical gifts. This attention greatly has bolstered his self-esteem, and as a parent, it fills me with pride. Music is a way for him to be socially accepted—to be encouraged and admired by his peers.

But it's important to also embrace, encourage, and applaud *all* of your child's accomplishments, no matter how small, because they probably haven't come easily to him. Sometimes, I was the only one who noticed the tiny changes other people would see as insignificant or even take for granted. I tried to help Josh recognize and feel that each step was progress! When he was little, he would recite lines from movies and memorize unbelievable amounts of information. As incredible as it was that Josh knew all of the lines from *The Lion King* at age 2, it was a day to remember when he shared something with us about himself! Josh and I always have had a very special bond. At times I could tell what he was thinking just from the look in his eye. I most certainly could tell if he understood what I was saying. I am filled with joy when I think of the unique connection we had when he was small. It is my hope that Josh will always know how much I love him, no matter where he goes, and that I hope others will somehow know him the way I do.

There have been many painful moments along the way as I've tried to do my best parenting my son. But there have been many more joyful times that make my heart sing and dance. The good far outweighs the bad.

Up until Josh was about 12 years old, whenever he would see me after school, he would run toward me at full speed with the biggest smile on his face and hug me with great enthusiasm. It was a very sad day when his therapist told him that it wasn't age-appropriate for him to do that anymore. I agree, but I still miss those days. We have to let our little boys grow up, don't we? But this is just a small nugget to give you a glimpse of the child I always have known.

Here's a story I frequently tell to help explain Asperger's to others: First, remember the subject in school where you struggled the most (for me it was physics)? You could learn it, but it was hard! Next, imagine walking into a room full of people. You see a person you recognize. Can you tell if she is happy or sad? In most situations you would say, "Of course, that's easy!" For Josh, it is the opposite. For him, school is easy, but he struggles with what we would consider "simple" social cues. That doesn't mean he can't learn those things, it's just that it sometimes is very difficult. Basic things such as eye contact, appropriate response, reading body language and interpreting a "sense of humor" all need to be taught.

In an episode of *The Big Bang Theory,* a friend asks Sheldon if he needs a sarcasm sign every time someone says something sarcastic (this is, of course, more sarcasm that Sheldon doesn't recognize).

Sheldon responds, "There's a sign!? That would be most helpful!!!" That explains how Josh views humor.

Josh is now a grown man and lives on his own. There are days when I wish he were closer so that I could help him through difficult times, or even help him see and celebrate the little advancements he makes each day. But, thankfully, Josh and I have a bond that was formed when he was small, so he still contacts me when he feels he needs help. There always has been a disparity between his actual age and his maturity age. This can prove to be challenging when the world thinks he should be acting one way, but you know that inside he is still a little boy. If only they knew him the way I do.

We tend to compartmentalize things to make them easier to understand. We most certainly want to know how to help our children, so diagnosis and understanding are powerful tools. Although there are certain similarities among kids on the spectrum, there also are many differences. Every year, more is revealed about Asperger's to inform our understanding that people with autism are *very* different from each other. My son said to me the week before he went to college, "Thomas Jefferson, George Washington, Dan Aykroyd, Steven Spielberg, Bill Gates, and Mozart all had Asperger's—and they did amazing things!" Our children on the spectrum may or may not change the world by being who they are, but they will definitely change the people around them.

Help the world to know that amazing, special child you know better than anyone.

Summary

Happily, you are raising the most incredible children ever. Undoubtedly, some of these stories resonate with you. Sometimes, we must teach the world how to treat our children, and sometimes our children teach us some truths about the world.

The parents in this chapter have illustrated for us the importance of advocating for their children. They refuse to let teachers mimic their child's walk or talk. They refuse to let their children be boxed in by a label. They refuse to let their children be compared to other children on or off the spectrum. Parenting on the spectrum requires that you recognize your child's special talents, abilities, and uneven developmental profiles. As parents you insist that others recognize the same qualities and honor them. Parenting on the spectrum requires that you find people who embrace your child, and that you make time for that bond to develop.

While you in your Superman cape are busy advocating for your child, your child is busy teaching you about life. These are the kids who remind us to celebrate victories, both big and small. They remind us to live in the moment. They show us a new depth of love and empathy— a completely new perspective. In the same way that kids allow us to shape them, we must let our children have the power to change us, as well, and thereby change the world.

six

The ASD Handbook Didn't Include This!
What Parents Wish They Had Been Told

Parents often wish they had a crystal ball that could help predict where their life, and that of their child, is heading. Unfortunately, we're not quite there yet. Until then, we will have to accept that life is an unpredictable journey accompanied with the usual travel companions: happiness, angst, loneliness, joy, and true friendship. For this chapter, parents were asked to identify the hard-earned wisdom they have now, what they wish they had known, and what gifts of knowledge they want to pass on to other parents at this point in their journeys.

Loneliness and Surprising Friendships

I wish someone had told me how lonely I would feel having a child with autism. I always had envisioned that parenthood would create an amazing social life. I am an extreme extrovert, so I was looking forward to the social aspect of parenting: gathering with friends and their children, meeting other parents at the playground, and watching our kids play together. I was looking forward to the summer BBQs, holiday parties, play dates, family sleepovers, and zoo trips.

Pretty early on, I realized that Logan saw the world differently. He came home to live with us when he was 3½ months old. At that time, he had been living in a foster home where he was left alone for long periods. Relying on himself for comfort, he would suck his thumb and scratch his face. By the time he came home to us he was so used to relying on himself for comfort that he refused comfort from me. He gave me very little eye contact, and would scream while lying on the floor. If I picked him up, the screaming just got more intense. I spent months on the floor next to him, trying to comfort him the best I could. Slowly, over time, he would tolerate more direct touch, first on his arms; I could get a hand under his back and scoot him closer to me. I would softly sing to him, often with tears streaming down my face, as I was grasping at straws on how to parent my son. I so desperately wanted to comfort him, but all the traditional ways of comfort were shocking and painful for him. Finally, after 6 months of slowly gaining his trust, I was able to comfort my son in my arms without his body being rigid. He finally was able to relax.

At 9 months, we took Logan to a developmental center for an evaluation. It was the first time anyone had mentioned developmental concerns. Logan was not babbling like a typical 9- to 10-month-old. He also wouldn't hold on to me when I was holding him on my hip. I filed those concerns in the back of my mind as we continued to watch him over the next several months. After his first birthday, I noticed that he never pointed at things; he wasn't connecting to the world around him, or at least not in a way that I could recognize. He was afraid of loud noises and would scream when people tried to interact with him. He spent most of his time playing with wheels on his trains and cars. He finally started walking around 16 months, and around that time, he started saying two words. I never had been so excited to hear a word as to hear him say "gup" for cup. Then, just as quickly as Logan's speech arrived, it was gone. After fighting with the regional center for several months, they finally evaluated Logan for speech therapy a few days before his second birthday. He qualified for speech therapy, and it was very exciting to see his progress over time. I was still in the dark about what might be making my son be so intense and impulsive, but I was so happy to see him learning words. It felt as if we finally were getting a glimpse into his personality.

Logan's early childhood was a lonely time in my life. My kids were very young: My daughter was 4, Logan was 3, and our youngest was an infant. My husband was in a doctoral program that was very demanding of his time. We lived in a small apartment, and the small task of going grocery shopping could send me over the edge. How was I supposed to get my three kids into the apartment with all the groceries when I had to park two blocks away, along a very busy street? The simple task of walking to the car was extremely stressful because Logan had a flight response to loud noises. A rumbling garbage truck or an emergency vehicle siren could send him running into a very busy street. Each trip out with my little family required a lot of frontloading and preparation, constantly reviewing my expectation that we would be holding hands the entire time. I would wear my youngest in a baby carrier, rely on my 4-year-old to be more mature than most kids her age, take Logan's hand, and finally we would attempt our outing. I am sure I looked like a crazed wide-eyed mom. In reality, I constantly was scanning our environment for potential triggers. Many times we had success; other times I would physically carry all three kids to our destination.

As our days continued to be long and progressed slowly, Logan's speech therapy led to an early childhood evaluation through the school district. At about the same time, we also were assigned a counselor through the regional center. The first day the evaluator came to the house, as Logan was crashing into all the furniture, throwing his body on the ground, and hitting me in the back with his head, he asked if Logan had autism. My heart sank. Nobody had said autism when referring to Logan, although they might have thought it. As difficult as it was to swallow at first, I felt a huge sense of relief. Maybe there was an answer to what we were experiencing. Getting that last evaluation was challenging. Our social worker through the regional center didn't think Logan was "that bad." I held my ground, and would not take no for an answer. By his third birthday, we had the diagnosis, and he was able to start preschool in an integrated classroom.

Early on, Logan had a lot of triggers. There were the obvious situations, such as loud noises, crowded spaces, and unpredictable kids on the playground. Then there were the subtle things that took me a while to figure out. If Logan saw a cup, he had to dump it. And if I kept him from dumping it? Instant meltdown. It didn't matter if it was a glass of wine or a plastic cup of water; he could not leave it untouched. After a few failed attempts at dining out (the poor patrons who had their glasses dumped!), we decided that eating out was not possible for our family. For some reason, the cup dumping got to me, mostly because I would get frustrated at myself for forgetting to put all cups out of reach or for forgetting to scan a room before entering. When you are struggling to parent under the best of circumstances, and your stress level is already high, a dumped cup of grape juice on the Sunday school floor can feel like the end of the world. My frustration led to my first creative solution in parenting Logan: I gave him five cups of water to dump each day. The deal was that he could only dump our special cups, and he had to leave all other cups alone. I am not sure if I got better at picking up cups, or if my compromise worked, but he is no longer dumping beverages.

About a year after Logan's diagnosis, we moved so that my husband could finish his doctoral program. I spent our first summer getting Logan set up with speech and occupational therapy. Logan was in therapy four days a week. Therapy was a huge time commitment, and worth every sacrifice. The wealth of knowledge I gained each week made me feel increasingly confident in parenting Logan. I was actively able to help my son succeed in the world around him. His occupational therapist (OT) gave me a set of tools (which I still use every day) to help Logan navigate through each environment. My previous strategies, such as letting him jump on a trampoline to release energy, had actually made our lives harder. Instead of calming him, such activities increased his energy level.

From our occupational therapist we learned why Logan loved to spin objects, and to spin his body: He was seeking sensory input. When he started spinning, the sensory need became our cue to swing him or offer some heavy work. Our OT also helped us manage meal preparation, which had been a huge chore because Logan was so impulsive he couldn't be left alone. We created tasks for Logan to work on at the kitchen counter while we made our meals. Some of his favorite tasks included sorting toy bugs and stuffing pom-poms into film canisters. He loved his jobs, and I loved the peace of mind. If I could recommend only one type of professional to another parent, it would be an occupational therapist.

Once Logan started kindergarten, we experienced a whole new set of challenges. Although there was a lot of structure within the classroom routine, there were many transitions throughout the day that were unstructured—and lack of structure plus Logan is a recipe for disaster. We were very fortunate that our neighborhood school had an incredible team of staff and teachers. Our integrated services team jumped right in with accommodations for Logan in the classroom. They gave him headphones (to control noise overload), a special chair for carpet time (to help define spatial expectations), and made sure that he always was the line leader (so that he had a clear place to be when it was time to line up). They also provided extra social support during recess and other unstructured time (to avoid meltdowns and promote peer relationships). I think Logan had a negative behavioral referral every other week, and my heart sank each time I saw the school number show up on my phone. I knew it was going to be a tough transition, and I knew that parents would stare at us on the playground as Logan screamed and kicked me during a meltdown. But what I didn't expect was the love and support I would feel. Here were people who saw my son at his worst. They never judged us, they never made Logan feel bad, and they worked with us as a team to figure out how best to support him. As the year went on, Logan had many successes. With each success, the entire team celebrated with him.

Today, Logan is in second grade. As we walk in to school each morning, arriving 5 minutes before the rest of the school to make his transition easier, you can hear many staff members and teachers welcoming him. Some mornings he might respond with a "hello," while other mornings he simply gives a grunt because it is all he can do just to get into the classroom without losing it. Whichever way he responds, everyone understands, and my husband and I feel relieved that we are not being judged and our son is not being labeled as rude. Although it might seem like a simple gesture on their part, their support has meant the world to us. Logan now has an environment where he feels safe, and his classroom teacher, special education teacher, and school occupational therapist advocate for him daily. They check in with me almost every day to let me know of any issues. We are in constant communication to ensure that we are using consistent language at home and at school. If he has an issue with a peer, the teacher lets me know so I can work with Logan to come up with a better way to handle a difficult situation. He and I often role play the scenario that happened on the playground, or in the classroom, and practice what he can do differently in the future. I try to give him as much social practice as possible in hopes that when he is stressed or overwhelmed, he will use the tools and solutions we have practiced.

I have cried many tears over autism. I have felt more alone than I ever could have imagined. I have watched friendships fade away, and I have felt the judging eyes of strangers. Autism can be isolating and scary. I also have felt more love and support than I ever imagined I would. I have watched people rally around my son, and I have watched a community come together and love our entire family unconditionally. There might not be summer BBQs, holiday parties, or sleepovers, but there is so much more. There are people who help me walk all three kids to where we need to go; and there are countless people who are willing to give us a hug on a particularly rough day. We are part of this community and no matter what happens, they will never let us be alone!

Sometimes Life Gets Harder Before It Gets Better

I wish someone had warned me that life would get frustratingly, mind numbingly, impossibly harder before it would get even the slightest bit easier. I first noticed that my son, Xavier, was "different" from his peers around his first birthday. He had developed the ability to wave goodbye and was beginning to say "Da-Da." Then suddenly, that stopped. He didn't mind if he was left alone to be with his toys. I say *be with his toys* because I also noticed he didn't *play* with his toys. He lined them up, sorted them by size, shape, color, and so on. I often found him on the floor with a car right next to his eye, spinning the wheel over and over again, and the whole time he was smiling and laughing to see it go around. He could do all of this, yet he spoke not a single word.

As Xavier entered the toddler stage, grunting and screaming became a part of our everyday lives. Such a simple thing as needing a drink often would end in one or both of us in tears because Xavier could not communicate that he wanted juice, not milk. To see your child cry over something as basic as a drink because he cannot get the words out is a daily gut-wrenching experience I would not wish on any child or parent. At home we learned to figure things out mostly by trial and error.

I started keeping journals of his "differences." Around the time Xavier was 19 months old, we paid a visit to a family member who educated me about the signs of autism. I instantly recognized that he was describing my son, without his ever having met my son. After that visit, I decided that if Xavier might have autism, it was my job to find him all the help he could possibly need to live a happy and fulfilling life—whatever that might look like or become.

I contacted my local Early Childhood Intervention Services and set up an appointment to have Xavier evaluated. It didn't take the specialists long to confirm what I now had been thinking for almost a year: My son was showing "classic" signs of autism, as well as sensory processing disorder. Soon afterward, the therapies began: occupational, physical, and speech. For 9 months, we had a different therapist in our house every other day, sometimes two, back to back.

We learned so much from those who came to help our son. These professionals each took the time to connect with Xavier, to bring him into our world and show him around slowly and gradually. We were in Xavier's world, and he was showing us around and teaching us how to do things his way. It was amazing that after struggling to learn to talk, to run, to hold a crayon, and to build a tower with his blocks rather than line them up on the floor, one day he finally looked at me when I called out his name. These people—total strangers—were helping Xavier and me find our way.

We learned to make a sensory bin with different things in it that would address his sensory issues. If he could calm his body, then he could focus on learning to communicate. Speech therapy was the greatest mountain we needed to climb, as Xavier had lost all speech. Our speech language pathologist (SLP) started with simple sign language, and within the first two sessions had Xavier using the sign for "more." This specific sign represented a huge step toward his verbal communication skills because it let us know that he understood us and what we wanted from him. Xavier did not speak verbally until just after he was 2½. The first word I heard him say was *more*. He wanted some more grapes, and instead of signing it, as he had been taught to do, he opened his mouth and out came *more* as he raised his bowl in my direction. I startled him when I burst into tears, snatched him up from his chair and almost smothered him in a bear hug ... but with that one word, our whole world changed.

I am eternally grateful for our speech therapist, Miss Anna. When Xavier was diagnosed, several professionals told me not to get my hopes up and to be as realistic as I could about Xavier's abilities to learn to talk. I was informed that he always would have deficits and not to focus on perfection, but rather to strive for completion. I'm still not sure what they meant by that last part. As an exception to these discouraging experiences, Miss Anna, our SLP, came for an evaluation and told me to not lose hope for my little guy. She reassured me that nothing was impossible and that she believed Xavier had it in him to succeed. With that in mind, we started teaching Xavier to communicate. Ultimately our goal was verbal speech, but if that's not how he chose to communicate, then we would explore as many other options as we could.

Sign language seemed to be the easiest place to start, as Xavier always had been one for using his hands in learning. In only our second session he used the sign for "more." Miss Anna was bouncing a ball, which always made him giggle at that age, and he wanted more bouncing! Slowly, but progressively, Xavier learned the sign for "please." I also was working with him at home; he loved to have me read to him. He could be running around like a crazed howler monkey, but if I picked up a book and sat down on the floor, Xavier was right there. I made sure to read to him and play flash cards with him. I pointed out everything we came in contact with and gave it a label for him. Most of the furniture in our house still has the paper labels I printed out and taped on them so he could learn that the spoken word had a written counterpart to the thing it labels—all that for a 2-year-old! I thought for sure that I was taking this too far; until he started school, that is.

Xavier's diagnosis qualified him to start school at 3. We were encouraged to enroll Xavier in a preschool program designed to support children with disabilities within our school district. I, however, did not want to send my 3-year-old to school for 7 hours a day. At the time, I believed such a long day was too much to ask of him. I was wrong.

It is difficult to teach something to children when they don't have the proper environment in which to learn. For example, I cannot teach Xavier to be social until he is in a social situation. It has to be taught on the fly; there is no other way. We practice his social stories all the time. Unfortunately, there's no way of teaching some situations until a kid is in his face, asking, "Why did you push me?!"

We would go to parks, the zoo, and other places with children; Xavier often was left alone because he wasn't driven to interact. I saw the potential for his happiness slip away because he wasn't being taught the skills he needed to desire interaction with the other kids. I couldn't stand the thought that I was preventing Xavier from reaching his potential, so I quickly changed my mind about school.

He started school the day after he turned 3; I cried so much that day. I cried because my son was among people who were going to help him be his best self. They wanted what I wanted for him, and they had the tools to do it. I cannot begin to say enough wonderful things about his teachers.

Soon after starting, it was clear that Xavier was thriving in his new environment. His language skills were growing rapidly; however, his social skills were now the main focus. As I just described, he didn't have the vocabulary needed to interact with other children in a social setting and most often resorted to physical behavior to get his needs met or his point across. This physical behavior, in turn, would cause children to avoid him.

After only 4 months in school, Xavier was potty trained: no accidents, no diapers … just like that. Within the first year of school, Xavier learned to read his own name and to say the alphabet.

I homeschool Xavier now; we just completed our first full year. The public school system did all it could, and more, for my son. Ultimately, the system is overburdened and underfunded. Homeschooling has nothing to do with the level of care I found in my son's teachers. It is what I believe to be the best for Xavier and our family. It has been 6 long years into our journey, with many more to go. I know now that as long I keep offering Xavier the chance to learn and grow, the sky is the limit. He is capable of great things and I can't wait to see what those might be.

What I Wish Someone Had Told Me Early On

I have been blessed with a wonderful, chaotic, loving, sometimes crazy family! My husband is a Marine, and we have two beautiful boys: Camryn, age 8, and Max, age 5. We are a military family, and that comes with a unique set of concerns. It's a different life from what typical families experience: With your spouse going on deployments and attending so many other trainings, only one parent is available to take care of everything at home. Being away from family and raising the kids without your better half isn't easy to begin with, and it gets even more challenging when you have kids with special needs. I don't think you ever get used to it, but you learn to manage.

Our story started like many others. We were living in Hawaii with Camryn, who was 2 at the time. After my husband returned from deployment, he noticed certain behaviors in Camryn that raised concern: spinning constantly, flapping when overstimulated, covering his ears when I would vacuum or for other loud noises, lining toys up over and over all day. I also noticed these behaviors, but with him being my first child, and with no outside input, I just thought that's how he played. We took him to see the developmental pediatrician, who confirmed Camryn's diagnosis; he was on the autism spectrum. His brother, Max, also regressed with his milestones: waving, pointing, and losing the two words he did say (*mama* and *dada*).

I felt that my world was spinning around me and I had no control over anything. I had so many questions and concerns about my son. Would he ever be able to talk, succeed in school, grow up to have a career, get married, or have kids? These thoughts circled in my head every day. I was scared, and no one could tell me much. Professionals were very vague about my son's future because there is no guarantee. Along with the lack of guarantee from professionals, we also had the bonus gifts of meltdowns and stimming when we left the house. An everyday moment that most people enjoy with their children was a task. A simple request for a preferred food was difficult for all parties involved. Grocery shopping was a daunting experience. We did not have the typical fuss at the store, but rather the screaming child in full meltdown, with everyone looking at me because they thought I was the "worst" parent for my methods.

It didn't help that Camryn always looked older than his chronological age. Once, when he was younger and still nonverbal, I actually had a woman on a plane ask me, "What is wrong with him?" and, "He is so old, he should be able to talk!" I politely said thank you and turned around. Fortunately, there were more compassionate people in our future.

During the period when Camryn was diagnosed, we received orders to move to North Carolina. I contacted the director of the school district's early intervention provider and enrolled Camryn in the program. I also scheduled therapies for occupational therapy, applied behavioral analysis therapy (ABA), speech therapy, and a program called TEAACH (Treatment and Education of Autistic and related Communication Handicapped Children). We had multiple therapies every day of the week. We also enrolled Camryn in military programs (extracurricular activities). Getting everything in place all at once was hard. Processing so much so fast was overwhelming. But having these therapies in place made me feel better knowing we were trying to be proactive.

When Camryn started therapy, he was completely nonverbal and unable to communicate his wants and needs. Thanks to early intervention services, he started communicating via the picture exchange communication system (PECS) and eventually began communicating vocally. Camryn's language expanded from one-word approximations to two-to-three word phrases, and then to using sentences to express his wants and needs. In addition, once he learned how to vocally express his wants and needs, his inappropriate behaviors decreased. He also learned how to follow directions, as well as to sit and do work for extended periods of time. These new skills led to a further increase in his skill acquisition (letters, numbers, shapes, colors, actions, adjectives, etc.).

Therapy also addressed pre-academic skills to help him prepare for school and learning in a typical classroom environment. Once in school, therapy goals focused on Camryn's completing his homework, which made him more independent and reinforced the concepts he was learning in school. Camryn made substantial gains. Eventually, the principal observing within the classroom did not know Camryn had an individualized education plan (IEP) or a diagnosis. Camryn's therapy hours have been decreased over time such that he no longer needs intensive therapy.

The most important lesson I learned is that you *always* will have to advocate for your child and what you think is best for him. Sometimes, you might be the only one who will. I was blessed to have our former ABA therapist with us for everything. She not only was his therapist, but she also helped *me* tremendously. Besides providing support inside the home, this therapist would accompany us on outings to help teach Camryn appropriate responses.

It was very difficult for me after Camryn's diagnosis and through-out his childhood. I beat myself up daily because I would see other kids developing so quickly; they were so far ahead of Camryn with respect to speech and other milestones. And it just got harder as he grew older. Don't get me wrong—I realize that every family has their own battles, and I wasn't looking for a pity party, but it still hurt inside.

However, when I look at Camryn now, I see a smart, loving boy who can do whatever he puts his mind to. It makes me happy that he has come so far! I know that all the work everyone put in has been worth it. And I know it's an ongoing process, but Camryn's future is more positive than it seemed 6 years ago.

I wish someone had told me that it was going to be OK! Here is my gift to you: hope. It can be hard to feel optimistic, but when you put together all of the interventions, therapies, and support, you do feel like it's going to be OK. It might sound corny, but keep having hope, and always advocate! Find out all the options that are available from your county, state, insurance company, and schools.

Summary

Generously, these parents are providing you with the gift they wish they had received in the parenting handbook: the missing chapters. Hard-learned lessons include the following:

- Therapy works. Your child will progress, continue to grow, *and* you likely will move mountains to get the right therapists in your child's life.
- Your social circles may change, *and* you will find there is no substitute for peer-to-peer interactions. You will make it happen.
- You will be lonely, *and* you will experience a depth of friendship unlike any other.
- On some days, you will feel isolated, *and* you will find a way to instill hope in yourself and in your child.
- Your best-laid plans will fail to materialize, *and* the plans you create instead will be nonlinear and more instructive than those of your wildest dreams.
- *and* you are raising the coolest kid ever.

Following are several good books on this topic:

- *Asperger's in Pink,* by Julie Clark
- *The Complete Guide to Asperger Syndrome* (aka "The Asperger's bible"), by Tony Attwood
- *Asperger Syndrome, The Universe and Everything,* by Kenneth Hall
- *Freaks, Geeks and Asperger Syndrome: A User's Guide to Adolescence,* by Luke Jackson
- *What I Wish I'd Known About Raising a Child With Autism: A Mom and a Psychologist Offer Heartfelt Guidance for the First Five Years,* by Bobbi Sheahan and Kathy DeOrnellas, PhD

seven

"I got this!": The Impact of ASD on the Family

So what is the impact of autism on the family? The chaos of autism promotes disharmony and divorce. At the same time, it has the potential to deepen your faith and your relationships with parenting partners. Autism can cause you to lessen your focus on your other children *and* create unique bonds among other people in the family. Most people wouldn't choose autism, but for those who have experienced the passion of a special interest, they wouldn't give it up either. Parents were asked to share the influence of autism on family life, including anticipated and unanticipated changes, positive influences, and the best part of the family dynamic.

Everything Changed

Last month was our annual checkup with our pediatric psychologist. We've made this trip for 3 years—quite often in the beginning, and now only annually. This year, as we left the appointment and walked out to the car, we passed another family entering the office building. As we loaded into our car and pulled out of the parking lot, my husband quietly asked, "Do you think we looked that bewildered at our first appointment?" I knew exactly what he meant, because I had noticed the same thing. While we had no idea what that family's purpose was at the office, we saw ourselves reflected in their faces.

Flashback to 3 years earlier. We always knew Jack was a little different from other kids his age. By the time we found ourselves sitting across from the psychologist in the winter of Jack's sixth-grade year, we already had drawn our own conclusions about what we were about to hear. So when the psychologist said, "Your son clearly falls within the parameters of autism spectrum disorder," everything changed and nothing changed, all in one moment.

As we drove home, Jack sat in the back listening to his music, blissfully unaware of the storm raging inside his parent's hearts and minds. Jack was at the meeting; he heard the doctor's diagnosis. However, unlike his dad and me, Jack appeared to be unaffected by the events of the afternoon. It was then that I had the realization that put everything into perspective: The 12-year-old boy who had just walked out of the doctor's office was exactly the same boy who had walked in an hour earlier. But we were not the same parents when we walked out of that appointment. Jack hadn't changed, but everything else certainly had.

For the first several months, my husband and I each processed the diagnosis in different ways. John withdrew into himself, reflecting quietly about embarking on this new path. He was the quiet voice of reason, always weighing pros and cons of any action we considered pursuing on Jack's behalf. I, on the other hand, was very external in my process. I sought out support groups, message boards, and online communities, always looking for a tangible plan of action. Together, we talked openly with Jack as well as his younger brother. We shared the diagnosis with family and close friends, building a network of support around our family.

We were now the parents of a special needs child. We became parents on a mission, no longer afforded the luxury of backseat parenting when it came to Jack's academic, social, and emotional health. One of the first steps we took was to work with the school to set up an individualized education program (IEP) for Jack. We had to advocate for his needs to be sure he was provided the best education possible. We sought out community support in the form of an equine therapy program. For 10 weeks, Jack participated in the program with a group of kids his age who also were on the autism spectrum, learning confidence-building skills such as self-regulation, calming techniques, and self-advocacy. We encouraged (and, if I'm being honest, sometimes forced) Jack to "stretch his social muscles" by becoming more involved in Boy Scouts. Because Jack doesn't play sports and would much rather spend his time in solitude watching YouTube videos, we set up the expectation of participation in scouting as a form of socialization.

Since choosing to become more purposeful with Jack's social and academic growth, we had to change the way we expected him to act in social situations as well as at home with the family. We became more patient, understanding, and compassionate than we had been before the diagnosis. Behaviors that were previously viewed as irritating—or infuriating—were now met with a desire to understand and gently correct. Instead of asking ourselves with exasperation, "Why doesn't Jack act like other kids his age?" we began looking for reasons behind the behavior so we could help him through it. Is he feeling anxious? Is it too loud/bright/chaotic for him to focus? Does he understand what is expected of him? Does he need a break to collect himself? Changing our expectations of Jack and acknowledging his strengths and limitations opened up a whole new way of parenting that we had never experienced. Our home became more peaceful, and our relationships with Jack improved.

Not every move we made was met with great support or success. I remember the time I showed up at a coffeehouse after finding out about a group of local "autism moms" who met monthly to offer support and encouragement to one another. I introduced myself, shared a little about my family, and then spent the next 30 minutes being completely ignored as they all complained to one another about their husbands, kids, and jobs. Not my idea of "support and encouragement."

Although our extended family and friends were, for the most part, completely supportive and helpful after the diagnosis, we've had our fair share of hurtful and sometimes shocking interactions with people. I had to block a distant family member on social media after she said ugly and hateful things in response to my post about the hardships of special needs parenting. Another time, upon introducing my husband and children to a coworker at a holiday party, he peered closely at Jack for a moment and then said loudly, "Funny, he doesn't look autistic."

Overall, despite a few bumps along the way, the past 3 years have been a time of tremendous growth for our family. We function more as a family unit now than even before, moving forward together with an understanding of one another that I don't think we would have had if not been for Jack's autism. Now, when we encounter another family about to walk through the same door of uncertainty and fear that we walked through 3 years ago, I hope they see peace and contentment reflected back at them through our experience.

Lessons From Living in ASland

Thirteen years ago, if someone had told me that I would have a child with autism, find out that my husband was on the autism spectrum, and that my life would be changed forever, I would not have believed it. After living in "ASland" (Autism Spectrum Land) for the past 12½ years, I'm finding that my idea of what is normal, satisfying, and rich has dramatically changed. I also realize that my life is far more complex and full than I ever would have guessed.

I sometimes am asked to talk about raising a child with autism. The challenge of such talks generally leads me to reflect on an essay written in 1987 by Emily Perl Kingsley. (The full text of *Welcome to Holland* can be viewed at http://www.our-kids.org/Archives/Holland.html.)

Ms. Kingsley wrote the now-classic piece that is handed around, parent to parent. The author describes what it would be like to get very excited about a trip to Italy, only to discover that the plane lands in Holland. After a brief grief-like adjustment, the traveler learns to enjoy Holland, sees Holland's strengths, and learns the language. Ms. Kingsley adeptly likens this imaginary experience to raising a child with special needs: Parents often have unspoken expectations about the parenting journey (the intended trip to Italy), read books about pregnancy and raising children, and then learn they are raising a child with special needs (here is where you envision an unexpected trip to Holland). In time, often after shock and grief, the parents learn to find the strengths in the child they have. Ms. Kingsley's piece addresses the grief and confusion that some people experience and the skill sets parents will learn—rapidly and by necessity.

With all due respect to Ms. Kingsley, when you find you have a special needs child, you're not just visiting, you've got to *live* in Holland and learn to adjust. Here's what you learn: The "travel agencies" (the professionals with whom you work) really do try to help, even if they can't understand what it's like to have to live in Holland. They can come to work and go home; we can't. Your neighbors who go to Italy don't know what Holland is like either—and they want to share their experiences in Italy. Sometimes, though, it's hard for them to understand our experiences in Holland; or they simply may not be interested in learning about how Holland is different. Although sometimes we have misunderstandings and know that things get lost in translation, we also know that we're all on a journey together and can share and learn from each other's experiences, regardless of which country we visit.

Our journey began when my son, Parker, was about 18 months old. At that time, I was still in graduate school training to be a psychologist and noticed that Parker's development simply stopped. His language development slowed and came to a halt, and at age 2, he was unable to "get" toilet training. He didn't walk until he was 16 months old. He would have intense meltdowns, during which he would kick, hit, punch, and bite; there were days when I went to school with bruises on my arms and legs from trying to keep him from hurting himself. I would have to try to restrain him, and he would injure me in the process. He began flapping his arms and banging his head ("stimming"). I kept telling our family doctor that I was seeing signs of autism, but we didn't get a referral until Parker was 2 years old. After a full psychological evaluation, he was diagnosed with mild to moderate autism. When we got the diagnosis, I was devastated. No one wants to hear that there is something wrong with her child. And because of my training in psychology, I knew that what I was seeing was autism; even so, the diagnosis took my breath away. To use the metaphor, this was when our plane changed course and landed in "Holland."

Along the way, we discovered that my husband also likely was "on the spectrum" (a phrase used to describe individuals with a diagnosis of autism spectrum disorder). As a child, he had speech delays, coordination problems, and communication difficulties. He also had extreme sensory food aversions that carry over into his life to this day. He and Parker share a decreased sensitivity to temperature. My husband used to be able to wear shorts in 10-degree weather! (Thankfully, that has passed.) He and Parker have other sensory sensitivities in common:

Neither can stand the feel of denim, and both are very sensitive to food textures. Both can be very rigid and "black-and-white" in their thinking, and both get easily overstimulated by noise and by crowds. This last sensitivity means that we tend to limit our outings to what they can handle, and depending on the environment, that might only be for a few minutes.

"Holland"—for my journey, let's call it "ASland" from now on—has its own language, customs, rules, and laws. First of all, the natives of "ASland" can be pretty touchy and irritable if you violate their customs and rules. Additionally, you don't always speak their language, and they can't communicate with you using the language you expect, so they get your attention in other ways. Meltdowns, hitting, kicking, and biting can be common occurrences.

However, once you learn to communicate with them, and the citizens of ASland learn to adjust to *your* customs to some degree, things get better, although "cultural misunderstandings" can and do continue to occur occasionally. After all, ASland's customs never completely will be your customs, and the rules in ASland always will be somewhat different from what you were used to. As you learn to live in ASland, your adjustment issues change: Teenagers and adults in ASland live their lives very differently from those who live in the neurotypical world. (*Neurotypical* is a term used to describe people who are not on the autism spectrum.)

Recognizing and interpreting social cues is extremely difficult, and misunderstandings are common. For example, recognizing that teasing is not always bullying is a very difficult concept. Misinterpreting an attractive person's nonverbal expressions and friendliness is common, as well; a smile can be interpreted as anything from "she thinks I'm hot and wants me" to not noticing it at all. This can be especially uncomfortable in the teen and adult years. It's not practical to have a "translator" interpret for you all the time, so misunderstandings, hurt feelings, and awkward social situations happen a lot.

The language of this country is something very different from what you're used to, as well. "ASlanese" is a language of color and of similes and metaphors. When Parker was a preschooler, I had a lot trouble understanding him: "I want the gray." "What's the gray, Parker?" "Like

Daddy takes pictures." "Oh, the camera!" Or "I go guffing." "Parker, what's guffing?" "Like Donald." (This is after thinking about things and remembering a distant episode of *Mickey Mouse Clubhouse*.) "Oh, you mean GOLFING, like Donald did!" "Yeah, Mommy—guffing!" The pronouns and syntax can vary, too: It's common to hear native ASlanese say, "You're not important to ..." to teach, to go to church, to work. What this really means is, "*It's* not important for you to ..." do any of these things; what it does mean is, "It's important for you to stay with me!" (But until you understand this, it's hell on your self-esteem!) Language differences continue no matter how long you stay in ASland. Even at 13, Parker still has problems with forming grammatically correct sentences or finding the right word for things. "Use your words" is still a common phrase in our family, and Parker still expresses himself a great deal through metaphors. "Macy's music," or "Starbucks music" are music genres in our family, and anyone who wasn't in on the lingo would be very confused. Songs on the radio or streamed are classified according to the businesses that might play them. Similarly, lights and architectural features are classified according to the familiar buildings in Parker's life: church, school, home, and his favorite shopping malls. This tendency continues to make conversation difficult at times. Recently, he was frustrated because I didn't understand how a building was "like church." It turned out that the beams on the ceiling were similar to the ones used in our church, and it took a series of clarifying questions to figure it out.

Second, the customs of this country are different from what you might expect. When we first landed in ASland, licking the walls and other objects (including people), sticking things in your mouth, repeating phrases over and over like a broken record were normal, even for a first- and second-grader. Using the toilet was *not* a given, as it is in other places, nor was looking at people when you talk to them or when they talk to you. Eye contact and toilet training are things that citizens of ASland have to learn to survive in our world, but it's not a given that it will happen on schedule.

Food difficulties are a particularly distressing issue; citizens of ASland have very particular, rigid, and sometimes odd food preferences. Traditional foods such as chicken and rice, fruit, or vegetables are shunned, and local favorites include peanut butter toast with ketchup or flavored tortilla chips with ketchup or barbecue sauce, or cheese, crackers and—you guessed it—ketchup. We buy peanut butter and ketchup in bulk. These differences make eating out very difficult; our choices usually are limited to fast-food restaurants or restaurants that can make accommodations. Holiday dinners generally are more stressful, and I find myself wondering every year if it's worth doing because every year I deal with the sulking, anxiety, and upset that comes with serving food that isn't liked. For my husband, anything raw, home-cooked, or unprocessed is nearly impossible to eat. Thus, our family tends to gravitate toward fast food and prepared and processed food from the grocery store. New foods and new restaurants are extremely stressful for Parker and for my husband, and this has limited our choices for trying new things. Even when we can, our choices are limited: Italian restaurants and places that serve burgers (fast food or otherwise) pretty much encompass our limited range. Chinese food, Thai, Mexican—we can't go to these restaurants because of my husband's and son's food aversions.

Third, recreational activities are different: Lining up objects is fun—and God help anyone who messes them up! Bouncing uncontrollably, flapping arms, or spinning around without stopping also are considered high entertainment. The "important things" in the culture include ceilings, escalators, elevators, lights and light poles, and "red balls," things to which most of us in other countries don't pay attention. (I found out recently that the "red balls" are called "marker balls." They are the balls on power lines that warn planes that the wires are there.) Buildings are an unending source of fascination. These are things that the rest of the world never notices, but because I get to see the world through Parker's eyes, I've learned that there is far more to the world than I ever knew. The cultural arts in ASland are different, as well. For a long time, Parker wouldn't allow anyone else to sing except him, unless it was church songs. Anyone else got, "You make my ears hurt!" Tact was, and is, not necessarily common in my ASland.

Play is different as well. For example, most kids play doctor, cowboy, firefighter, teacher, and so on. Parker used to play "pastor," where he gave sermons and reiterated the practices of our church.

He imagines being a cashier. His art is very different from that of most children; where others draw houses, trees, and people, Parker will draw floor plans of his favorite stores and places, complete with lights. Our walls are covered with what look like blueprints of various stores and places (the library, department stores, or the Budweiser Event Center in Loveland, CO). Since he's discovered games such as Minecraft, he has been able to take his floor plans to a three-dimensional view. He recently built a virtual hotel, including lobby, conference center, atrium, and each room, all containing lights and furniture.

And my favorite activity? Parker has to ride the escalators at Macy's for at least an hour before it is OK to go enjoy the rest of our Saturday ... because "riding the escalator is *cool*, Mommy!" At age 13, he continues to be fascinated with escalators, elevators (and their buttons and manufacturers), power poles, lights, and blueprints of buildings. I now know the manufacturers of pretty much every elevator company in the world and have concluded that power poles talk to each other, get married, and have feelings.

I've learned that routine is critical, for both children and adults, and when that routine is changed, I risk seeing all hell breaking loose. Activities that are common in other "countries," such as taking vacations to new places, produce incredibly high levels of anxiety for natives of ASland. When my husband gets irritated and upset in unfamiliar environments where his preferences may be challenged, I have learned that it's time to leave. The same is true for Parker. Otherwise, I risk dealing with sulking, a tantrum, and/or nasty comments later (depending on who is uncomfortable). Although huge meltdowns no longer are as common as they used to be with Parker, there still is a risk if he is overstimulated or bored. Puberty has brought about meltdowns again; adolescence with an autistic child is new to me. My husband won't have a meltdown in public, but he makes his displeasure extremely obvious once out of the public eye.

I've also learned to ignore the whispered comments from people who are not familiar with ASland: "Why can't she control that child?" "What's wrong with her—what did she do wrong with him?" "What's wrong with her? I'd never let my kid behave like that." "She should get him out of here. What was she thinking?" And as much as I try to ignore the comments, or try to help others understand, these comments and judgments still hurt. I understand, though, because I realize that I probably have done the same at times and thus try to remember to be more compassionate toward other parents when I feel this way. However, I've learned to be more assertive and to advocate for Parker's rights and needs; our "neurotypical culture" is not very understanding, supportive, or even tolerant of people on the spectrum.

Like all parents, those of us with special needs children are diverse in many ways. But at the same time, we have a lot in common. When we find each other, we "get it" on a level that parents of neurotypical children will never quite understand. Our families learn to adjust, and when neurotypical children also are part of the family, our kids on the spectrum have to learn to adjust, as well. When Parker's neurotypical sister was born, her presence in his life and her reaching developmental milestones on time helped Parker reach those milestones as well. Parker is a very competitive person, and I believe he saw her as competition. That she was very verbal and social helped him, as well. When Parker would try to withdraw, she wouldn't let him. (She's very stubborn!) When she learned to open gifts at 1 year old, Parker saw her and did the same. He had not figured it out until her first Christmas when he was 3. Her eating habits, her neurotypical and advanced development, and her very social and verbal personality pushed Parker to catch up developmentally.

I've learned that it's not all hard, exhausting, or tough. There are moments when the true wonder of these amazing individuals shines through. I never, ever take Parker for granted; I notice, appreciate, and celebrate every achievement and every reach toward growth (although I will admit that puberty and preteen angst have been challenges). Every developmental milestone he reaches, no matter how late, is cause for joy and gratitude. I have found friends, family, therapists, school services, and groups to support Parker and our family when we're down, to help him grow and thrive, and to be there when we need them. Having people try to understand and be supportive helps more than anyone will ever know.

And, every now and then, this child amazes me. Although he can be a handful some days, on other days, he'll astound me with his caring and sensitivity. He'll argue with his sister for days on end, but then give her his coat when she has forgotten hers. He will stick up for children who are being bullied, and he will stay close to family members when they are upset. Parker is very protective and loving toward me, even as an adolescent. He doesn't have many friends, but he is strongly connected to the friends he does have. He has developed close relationships with peers, teachers, and friends, and he tries new things now that he never would have tried without support. For people who believe that individuals on the spectrum don't feel emotions, I'd like to tell them, "You have no idea." My husband and Parker are two of the most sensitive people I know, and at times they can be two of the least self-aware people, as well. Although they may have difficulty expressing how they feel or communicating those feelings, they *do* feel things. Oh, they feel things deeply.

The bottom line is that living in ASland has changed me. Our family is different. My world has been both restricted and enhanced in ways that I never could have guessed. I experience frustrations most people don't understand, and I appreciate things that nearly no one else would notice or that most people would take for granted. Parker and my husband have taught me to see the world in a very different way than I ever would have on my own. My life might have been easier without family members on the autism spectrum, but I wouldn't trade it for the world. Yes, there are things that make me want to scream with frustration, and there are things my husband and son do that drive me crazy. There are days where I feel like I can't take it anymore. As a result, I've learned to adjust both my actions and expectations, and have learned to appreciate the world and my family in a new way. I can't imagine what life would be like now without Parker. He is a gift, as is my husband, and my life is far richer because they are in it. I and my neurotypical family members have stretched and grown in ways we never could have predicted, and I wouldn't give it up for anything.

References

Crawford, L. K. (n.d.). *Holland, Schmolland.* Retrieved from http://www.autism-pdd.net/testdump/test16481.htm

Kingsley, E. P. (1987). *Welcome to Holland.* Retrieved from our-kids.org/archives/Holland.html

Life Is What Happens When You're Busy Making Plans

Family dynamics has been defined as "the forces at work within the family that produce particular behaviors or symptoms" (The Free Dictionary, n.d.). That definition struck me as funny to start with because our family dynamic was changed by behaviors and symptoms, not the other way around.

I have wanted children for as long as I can remember. I loved being with children, and I thought I'd be good at motherhood. There were so many "wrongs" committed against children I thought I could "right" in my own experience. I waited a long time to have children and to share them with the right man. I was 31 when we got married, and our firstborn came when I was 38. We had tried for 9 months before we got pregnant, and there wasn't a baby born more loved, more obsessed over, or more wanted.

When our second son, Jordan, was born, our older son, Ryan, was 22 months old. Those years were the best season of my life as I nurtured and cared for those little babies.

Like a lot of parents, we had certain expectations going into parenthood, which were shattered by the eventual diagnosis of autism. My expectations weren't grand or ambitious, just that my children would know that they were loved, safe, and free to explore the world. I wanted to give them a wonderful childhood. I wanted to expose them to as many different cultural, intellectual, physical, spiritual, and natural experiences as I could, so that they would know what the world had to offer. They could choose from those experiences and develop their passions. I assumed that I would see them off into adulthood with the tools they needed to live lives of purpose and color.

Jordan was a beautiful baby. He didn't do anything on schedule, so there was plenty to obsess over. He had weak trunk muscles, so he crawled late and then walked late. But he started talking at 14 months old. His first word, after *mama* and *dada*, was *lawnmower*!

By contrast, Ryan hit all his physical milestones right on time but didn't start talking until his second birthday. The two children were different in their own ways, but being in the thick of the parenting journey, there wasn't anything in particular that set off alarm bells in my head—until Ryan reached 3 years of age. He continued to progress just fine physically, but cognitively he just … stopped. I remember his 2-year well-check. The doctor always wanted to know my concerns, and the only one I really had was that Ryan didn't have many words. The doctor's answer was that there was a wide range of normal, that boys typically talk later than girls—in other words, nothing to worry about. At his 3-year well-check, where it was expected that he would have 50 to 100 words, he had 10. With everything else looking normal, I again was told not to worry.

I was working part time, and my children were being cared for by my mother-in-law. One day, quite unexpectedly, she said that she found a woman who was starting a home day care. She had a master's in social work, with a minor in early childhood development. My son would be her first customer; she had her own two little girls at home with her. She lived close to my job, and she was OK with part time. I thought that my mother-in-law was just tired.

After about a month of having Ryan in her care, the woman started voicing concerns about him. For example, when they tried going on walks, he would run out into the middle of the street and not respond when she called his name. She said that despite her repeating the rules of the house to him, he kept breaking them. She said she was getting frustrated, and she wanted things to work because she really loved him. We kept talking and trying different things, but in the end, she said she just couldn't care for him. I thought that she was just not used to boys. Or that she was expecting too much of a 3-year-old. Or that his being there every other day, with the alternate days being at home, were just too confusing for him. We certainly did not see an ASD diagnosis coming.

While we were waiting for Ryan's assessment appointment, I talked to my friend, an occupational therapist. Based on what she saw and what I described to her, she said it seemed to her that Asperger's syndrome fit. I looked it up, and I thought, "OK, he'll be quirky and socially awkward, but he will live, and he will be able to function in the world." But when I left the hospital after receiving the autism diagnosis, I thought, "This is all he'll ever be."

Upon reflection, we were a tight-knit family moving in the right direction and making intentional choices. My husband had finished college and had a good job. I was planning to scale back my work life so that I could stay home with the kids. We had moved to beautiful Colorado. We were in love with our kids and with each other.

It was a big shock to find that Ryan was struggling. The challenges he presented with did not look so far out of place for a 3-year-old boy. Looking back, I had precious little time with them before we had to make a major shift in our approach to parenting, our expectations, and our dreams for their lives.

I anticipated that life would change. I always have been forward-focused and a problem solver. I knew that we would have to educate ourselves but that we would find answers. I thought that surely there would be help out there for us.

I never thought I would become a 24/7 caregiver. I didn't think I would become an expert in autism symptoms, behavioral therapy, and medical and holistic interventions. I didn't know I would earn a PhD in "Life on the Island of Sodor" (a fictional island in the Irish Sea, most recently referenced in *Thomas the Tank Engine*).

However, I'm now glad to say I was wrong about my initial worries that Ryan never would progress. He has made a good many strides from that day to now. For instance, he went from being practically nonverbal—having to put his finger on pictures to make his needs and his wants known—to being quite a talker. I have every expectation that he will continue to make strides and will continually surprise us. Our work, though, never will be done!

The biggest change that caught me off guard was when he turned 18. Until then, Ryan had been pretty much the same person. For the most part, I could manage his behaviors. I could encourage him, get him to try new things, and teach him. After turning 18, Ryan is fully into his willful teenagehood, and it is a challenge to redirect him. Add that he's now more than 6 feet tall and 220 pounds, and he's really quite a handful!

Jordan's challenges were much harder to spot, and harder to take. We knew we had one special needs child, but we thought the other one was doing pretty well. You just could not compare the two to each other: Ryan was disabled in the very definition of the word. He required one-on-one supervision, and we expected that to continue for his entire life. Jordan was (and is) smart, articulate, capable, and social—all the things Ryan was not. It took us a long time to get to the point of diagnosis, and when we did, it was shocking on a grander scale.

Jordan's challenges came to the forefront when he entered eighth grade. I had decided to homeschool him starting in second grade so that we could have dedicated time together, just the two of us. Counter to the popular arguments against homeschooling, he had plenty of socialization. At 13, Jordan decided he wanted to go to a "regular" school, and we agreed. I found a charter school I really liked and thought would be a good fit for him. We enrolled him.

Over time Jordan's struggles got harder and harder, and his social struggles were getting harder to ignore. Jordan's life had become unmanageable, and in an effort to help him, we had him assessed as well. Jordan received a diagnosis of Asperger's disorder. Since then, I have been trying to manage problems and crises on two fronts. Parenting two children on opposite ends of the autism problem is quite a challenge.

I would say that our family dynamic has changed in immeasurable ways. It has stretched us as people, and given us insights we wouldn't be aware of had we not had this experience. My husband and I are survivors. We are strong. This journey has taken its toll on us personally and on our marriage. We're still together because we truly care for one another, and we love our children. Nevertheless, I understand why the divorce rate for parents of special needs children is 80%. In our worst moments, we've certainly considered it.

If I had the benefit of hindsight, there are things I would change. I think I would have moved heaven and earth to get Ryan into a specialized school for autism. He had a public school education from preschool to eighth grade. It was only of intermittent value, however, despite the best efforts of many caring people along the way who were able to help him in various ways. What Ryan needed, what so many of these kids need, was intensive and comprehensive intervention.

I also would have paid more attention to my intuition. When we were navigating the world of professionals, I looked to them for guidance. I wanted and needed to have someone say, "We know what this is. We know what to do. Here's the plan." There were times when I felt in my heart that we should go in other directions, but I let the "experts" sway me. Looking back, I wish I'd been more of a fighter and an advocate.

With my older child, I think my "lessons learned" fall under the heading of anticipation. Jordan did not get the childhood he should have, the childhood he deserved. From the moment his brother was diagnosed, our lives revolved around the younger one's needs. Sometimes that was by design; sometimes it was demanded of us by his behavior. We tried in different ways to "make it up to him." My husband and I were intentional about each spending time with him alone and having dedicated time for the three of us, as well as family times.

When Jordan was diagnosed with Asperger's, I wish I had been more aware of his struggles. He had been diagnosed with ADD/ADHD in first grade. Other than that, he functioned so well for so long that I thought his struggles were just part of his personality or a reaction to his brother. It turns out that that wasn't the case.

The core of our family is my husband and myself. I think we are uniquely qualified to do this job, even though it is not something that we chose, would have chosen, or would even choose again if it were up to us, knowing all that we know now.

At the heart of who we are, though, we have strengths that serve us well. First and foremost, we are people of faith. Our Christian faith and our walk with God are so important to the both of us. Without His love, strength, mercy and grace, and our ability to access Him in our daily lives, I don't see how we could have made it this far. After 25 years, we are still married, still tending our little family garden. We lack the strength within us to accomplish this alone.

Second, we are both problem solvers. When presented with something as devastating to our hearts as these diagnoses, our approach was, and still is, "OK, this is what we're dealing with. Now what do we do about it?"

Third, we are open. Open to new ways of looking at a problem, open to new ways of thinking, open to learning about ourselves. We are big believers in therapies of all kinds. We've been to couples counseling, individual counseling, and family counseling. We know there are some hills we can climb, and some we can't. There are times and issues that need outside consultation with someone who is objective.

We have been enormously blessed to have the support of our extended family. Between the two of us, we have six parents. They all have been supportive and helpful. My husband's mother, in particular, because she lives close to us and has watched Ryan for long and short periods so we can get a break. She is the only one I really trusted to keep him for overnights, and that has been a huge blessing. My cousin and his wife have agreed to be his guardians should something befall my husband and me. Our close friends, who are like family to us, also have welcomed Jordan with open arms and infinite patience.

The parenting road has its full share of peaks and valleys. That is true of everyone. I often hear the phrase, "God gives these children the parents they need." On the good days, I think, "Yeah, that's right!" On the bad days, I'm not so sure. I think about the variety of ways in which people with autism suffer, and the gifts that they give. My son, Ryan, always has been a "hugger;" he never screamed or arched away from my touch. For that, I'm grateful. He has empathy, a quality with which many individuals on the spectrum struggle. For that, I also am grateful. His achievements take on so much more significance because of how hard he has to work to get there. My children exist in a world that is not made for them. I think it's the world that needs to change.

Reference

The Free Dictionary. (n.d.). "Family dynamics" definition. (n.d.). Retrieved from http://medical-dictionary.thefreedictionary. com/family+dynamics

Summary

What is the impact of autism on the family? Your relationships *will* change in substantial and unpredictable ways. You may find your faith (and your patience) tested and strengthened. You may find strength inside yourself that you never envisioned. You may develop cognitive flexibility in ways your friends and family members never could anticipate.

Autism will test you, and we think you will surprise yourself with your own strength.

Resources to support this topic include the following:

- *The Journal of Best Practices: A Memoir of Marriage, Asperger Syndrome, and One Man's Quest to Be a Better Husband,* by David Finch
- *Autism in the Family: Caring and Coping Together,* by Robert A. Naseef, PhD
- *A Friend's and Relative's Guide to Supporting the Family With Autism: How Can I Help?,* by Ann Palmer

Step III

Your Future Journey

eight

The Question of the Century:

Where Is Your Child Headed In Life, and How

Will He or She Get There?

Anyone with children wonders about their future. Parents were asked to ponder questions such as the following: Where will my child live? What will he do? How will she afford her life? Who will love him? And who could possibly love her as much as we do? These are poignant lessons for all families, and are magnified for families raising children on the spectrum.

What Will Miss T Do?

When we began this journey nearly 8 years ago, we had no idea what can of worms we'd opened. I will be the first to admit that I think the proverbial worms are probably more closely related to those from the movie *Tremors* than your average night crawlers. Not to say that things have been bad and scary, just wholly unexpected, and at times earthshaking. But that's the beauty of people with Asperger's: Not one of them is like the other.

Now that we are in Miss T's freshman year of high school, we can look back at some of the incredible things she's grasped: pragmatics, social skills, and fine motor skills. She also has mastered some behavioral quirks. She's always had a fierce spirit, which we have strongly supported. She's more assertive at 14 than I am at 37. When faced with a sticky situation, many times I ask myself, "What would Miss T do?"

So that's the question of the century for us. Or rather, "What *will* Miss T do?" She is talented in so many areas, the most notable being art. She's shown interest in fashion design, special effects makeup (some seriously wicked gory stuff like in *The Walking Dead*), and, my personal favorite, being her own boss. Miss T absolutely devoured my copy of the book *Girlboss* by Sophia Amoruso and is certain she will lead her own tribe. She isn't content to own a mere small business. She wants an empire. And minions. Because of her strong spirit, we tend to agree that being her own boss is probably the best for her. While loving and kind, Miss T also can be stubborn, taking no prisoners. She usually does pretty well when it comes to doing what teachers ask her to. But when she runs into a teacher she doesn't like, there is no hiding it.

We worry about how this might affect her career. She fixates on how she wants to do something, and nobody can tell her differently. How will that fly with a boss down the road? I guess there's only one way to find out. But, in the meantime, I hope taking business classes in high school will help her understand business etiquette, whether it's at a place she works or a place with her name on the front flashing in neon (and possibly glitter cannons).

Miss T has an individualized education program (IEP), and, starting in ninth grade, we've been narrowing in on potential career paths for her. She attends an arts magnet school, where they integrate fine art, creative writing, theater, and dance into core classes. This is how she communicates, and even though very few of her classmates in this program are autistic, they all have artistic hearts. They thrive on drama, beauty, and all things creative. They speak the same language, even if they have different dialects.

In addition to art classes, we are encouraging classes in home economics, marketing, business, and health. For her to truly be her own boss and to be able to make a successful living, she needs to master these skills—not only to balance her books, but also so others do not take advantage of her. More on that later.

She's already told us she'll go to college. She'll definitely start at a community college, where class sizes are small and where she won't feel lost, as she might as one of hundreds of students in introductory courses at a university. She may or may not live at home while she's doing these first few years. Miss T is a fearless wonder, but I still think it's important that she not jump into adulthood all at once. Aspies tend to need baby steps and to take time to adjust to new things. Once she's ready, she'll finish her degree at the university. She wants to major in graphic design and minor in business, and we know she's going to rock both of them.

Lately, Miss T has made it clear that she wants nothing to do with an IEP or special classes. She doesn't want special treatment, to be singled out, or for anyone to have a clue that she needs accommodations. Her high school teachers and other staff have been great at honoring her wishes and being discreet. She does her best to blend in with what everyone else is doing, but still lets her light shine. People think she's funny and quirky, and as an adult, she'll probably be considered artsy and eccentric.

As for college, she is entitled to accommodations if she needs them. However, with her stubborn streak being a hundred miles wide, I don't know if she'll take advantage of them. And I will sit in the corner, biting my tongue, repeating the mantra, "I will not be a helicopter parent" over and over and over again, until muscle memory forces my lips to only form that phrase. It's all good.

Miss T has a long way to go with life skills. Right now she's having a hard time understanding why the things she wants don't magically appear when she asks for them, or why we have to say no when she wants the latest iPhone. Budgeting is for losers.

These are all lessons she doesn't want to hear from her parents: We've tried, but we don't know anything! So we have evil plans in place to ensure she hears it from somebody credible. We are fortunate that one of her favorite teachers at school teaches a few classes on life skills, and Miss T's counselor is going to give her preference for those classes. She has 3 years of high school left as I write this, and we can only hope that she will graduate with realistic expectations for adulthood. My husband and I will smile and nod when she tells us all the great things she learned about those subjects from her teachers at school. And we will *not say a word.*

The financial lesson is multifaceted. While we often explain budgets, savings, and how to spend money wisely, these are concepts she still is struggling to grasp. She knows she wants to save half of the money she earns through allowance, babysitting, and face painting, and the other half is her fun money. Many times she will make impulse buys on things that are ... quite interesting. Case in point: She has a brand new shark onesie, and I'm dying to see where she plans to wear it! I hope not to church. But I'm sure Jesus loves sharks, too.

The other side of making money is earning a living. She's going to have to work steadily, to balance her books, and to pay bills on time. Through therapy we've learned to find good incentives to do things she doesn't like to do, which works for a while. But sometimes she decides that whatever it is she's supposed to do is just not her thing. She'd rather accept the consequence for not doing it than to gain the reward of doing it and moving on.

She's going to have to self-motivate once she's on her own. If she doesn't work, she doesn't eat—and she can't feed herself on shark onesies—but she plans on buying a mansion and getting her friends to rent rooms from her so that she can afford her sweet lifestyle. The concept of a credit history is way over her head at this point. Her plan is to earn so much on rent she won't have to get a day job. I like slumlords just as much as the next person, but for every realistic concern I present to this plan, she has a solution. Usually, it involves more minions.

Also concerning to me is her tendency to buy things for her peers while on field trips or from the concession stand at sporting events, and when it's time to buy her own meal or admission ticket, she won't have anything left for herself. And her "friends" many times don't return the favor. I've gotten many frantic calls from Miss T saying she doesn't have any money for a $5 ticket after I sent her in with a twenty. She is kind and takes care of people, but sometimes she doesn't take care of herself.

But my biggest concern for when Miss T leaves the nest is self-care. We have no problem with hygiene and fashion choices (for the most part). But those pale in comparison to the bigger picture. I lose sleep worrying about whether she'll keep up with her prescriptions, psychology and psychiatry appointments, stress management, and so on. What if she decides to stay up all night doing something she thinks is important at the time, only to sleep through work or an exam? What if she has a bad breakup and slides into permanent meltdown mode?

What if she burns bridges with important people in her life and is too stubborn to apologize?

What if, what if, what if?

Relationships take work. When she adores somebody and feels motivated to keep the friendship, she will move mountains for that person. When she has a friend who laughs inappropriately at something she said, she relegates the offender to the acquaintances column. When she's mad at somebody, she will never, ever, forget what that person did to her, and she won't hesitate to bring the infraction up when she's mad at him or her again. But when it comes to accountability for her own actions, she won't apologize unless she has to get something else she wants. Grudgingly.

It's the two-way-street concept that's going to be a big challenge.

Parents are forgiving and have that whole unconditional love thing going. Even as adults, some friends might not be so understanding. Coworkers and bosses will be even less so. Over the next few years of high school, these are the biggest things we will be working on. Miss T must acquire the ability to politely and professionally communicate, even if it hurts. If she is her own boss, she'll still have clients to keep happy and take care of her "minions" in more ways than just a paycheck. She plans to work through high school, so some of these early jobs will be good practice for her.

We have little doubt that she will be able to live on her own as an adult, as long as she can figure these things out over the next few years. Her brain is still maturing, and she still has teenage impulses, which are hard enough to navigate for neurotypical kids!

Something my husband and I discussed with our financial planner is the contingency that we might have to financially support her. We have to build that into our life insurance, retirement, and savings plans should the unfortunate happen. Somebody probably will have to act as executor to make sure she has a financial allowance and not blow our fortune all at once on onesies. If Miss T decides not to marry, we want to make sure somebody checks in on her to ensure she's keeping up on self-care.

She has vacillated on the topic of love and a lifelong partner several times. She doesn't usually paint the white picket fence picture of a husband and two kids. Depending on how her relationships have gone that day, she'll either decide she's going to adopt a bunch of kids and raise them Madonna style or have a significant other and go the more traditional route. Many days she has said that nobody will ever love her.

But *we* love her. And we will be there for her throughout all of this, no matter what choices she makes. As parents we have to guide, but not make decisions for, our children with Asperger's. We have to teach them to make their own decisions, to think logically, to learn to weigh good versus bad decisions, and to seek out the gray area in between. Planning, contingencies, troubleshooting—all are things that are hard to grasp for our black-and-white–minded kids. If they struggle with that, we can be there as sounding boards, good listeners, and disaster managers, if need be.

We can't predict the future, but we do need to think ahead. We need to learn our kids' strengths and their not-strengths, and learn what we can do as parents to encourage a productive adulthood. And, hopefully, we will guide our kids to a place where they feel a modicum of personal success.

In the meantime, do your homework. Buckle up. And bring a clean pair of underwear. You're going to need it.

Helping Him Find His Own Path

For parents of children with ASD, no matter the children's place on the spectrum, expectations of their future paths always are at the forefront. There isn't a single day that passes without the permeating thought of "What's next?" Variations of this question can rattle your very being and bring you to question, and want to change, every decision you make.

Our job as parents, in part, is to ready our children for the challenges and opportunities they will face in life. The good and the bad news is this will look different, yet still familiar, for every family on this journey. One size definitely does not fit all.

Now 11, our son, Jagger, is racing toward adulthood, with curiosities to match. It's time to face bigger life questions and help him understand the hows, whys, and whats, even if we have no earthly clue as to what to say. A sense of humor is necessary to stay focused and grounded in reality. The future is always what you make of it, and that doesn't change because of a diagnosis. Or at least it shouldn't.

There are two different sets of hopes to think about and nurture: those of your child and your own. For our child, we hope for happiness and the love and patience of a partner and friends. We hope for compassion from strangers and support from communities. We hope that our kids will have the tools they need to thrive in an unforgiving world. We hope that people stick up for them in appropriate situations. We hope for their ability to make decisions. Much to our heartfelt opposition, we hope for their freedom and ability to live on their own, with assistance, if needed.

We also think about personal struggles unique to our kiddos. We worry about how they will continue to work through these struggles when we aren't there to help. That's some serious long-term worrying right there. With learning delays and differences, every child progresses at his or her own pace.

For instance, at 11, our son just gained the confidence needed to attempt to cross the street by himself. On the way to piano lessons, we have to cross a fairly busy street with multiple visibility obstructions. As I often do, I asked him if he would like to learn how to cross the street on his own. Up until this past year, the answer to these types of questions would typically be along the lines of, "Nah, I think I'm too young and it would be inappropriate." This year he found the courage to cross the street independently. Ironically, initially it required me walking directly beside him. Then he suffered through several equally nerve-racking attempts while I watched and coached. One day, Jagger got out of his piano class early, and since my shop is directly across the street from his piano lessons, he decided to cross without me. He came bounding through the doors, smile a mile wide, and loudly proclaimed, "Dad! I did it. I crossed the street by myself!" We hugged and had a moment. He enthusiastically texted his mom with the news. This was a huge deal in our lives and one we celebrated. He now takes himself to and from piano lessons once a week. While this may give his mom a little anxiety every Monday morning at 10, it's a necessary lesson in independence.

We hope he continues to grow as a person and that he seeks out opportunities for growth. As a rule follower, Jagger tends to feel most comfortable within a certain set of uniquely defined boundaries. We make sure to push him outside of those boundaries whenever it seems appropriate. It's not always his favorite thing, but he usually ends up appreciating something about the experience.

One thing that is and always will be a struggle is social interaction, which I think is the most common and misunderstood trait for any-one on the spectrum. In my opinion, the Western world is producing far fewer socially aware individuals as a result of the increased use of electronic devices as interaction tools. More than ever, the need to improve social skills is intensifying. As a result of the tech boom, we are losing opportunities to teach these skills with peer groups.

To help Jagger learn social skills, we always have pushed him to do activities with neurotypical peers. When we realized at an awkward Christmas dinner that the boy was lacking in social mealtime graces, we found a local cotillion and signed him up.

Now, I have to be honest: I am somewhat socially awkward myself. OK, I'm all-the-way awkward. Something like a cotillion is absolutely ter-rifying to me, even at my advancing age. I mean, at 11 years old in full-on puberty, getting all dressed up to be taught social lessons with the opposite sex? I would have awkwardly fainted in the presence of girls.

Right before his first cotillion class, although Jagger was extremely nervous and really disliking wearing a tie and button-down shirt, he also was excited. It was great to see the anticipation of doing well push him through the first class. The clincher seemingly was when we told him that he would learn how to dance with girls his age. He danced with fervor, spoke with a soft confidence, addressed adults formally, introduced his partner, and ate a four-course meal by himself using these newly learned skill sets.

This cotillion experience was invaluable, and he is even looking forward to it again next year. Once Jagger was able to see other kids his age having to do the same thing, he joined and modeled. Gently pushing him outside of his predefined, strict boundaries has been the basic principle behind everything we do. He needs it. We keep him on target and gently call him on it when it starts to slip.

This is where a lot of education, patience, and simple explanations will help. Puberty has opened up all kinds of new and terrifying questions and statements.

A concern we have, and a skill we try to nurture, is openness in communication. It's very hard to "read" him and to successfully interpret what he needs. At the same time, we realize that we now need to introduce the concept of privacy and discretion. Suddenly, we need to make "invisible rules" about privacy and discretion tangible, and that is a very challenging series of conversations.

When we think about the future, I don't think Jagger's issue will be how to love. He seems to have that concept down in its most precious and purest form. Actually, I have noticed this trait among many kids with ASD I've come to know over the years. Their level of compassion reaches heights I've personally never achieved. Or at least not as often. It's inspirational.

For our kid, it's not how to love. It's how to function within a relationship and navigate the intricate dynamics. How is interpersonal functioning defined and by whom? Sometimes it's the most basic thing, like making sure you say "hi" to everyone in a room, or knowing when it's OK to start eating at a family dinner. Or knowing when and how it's appropriate to end a phone conversation. Significant attention to detail is needed to learn the basics, but that doesn't imply nuance. Once the "basic rules of engagement" are cemented, they are truly cemented. You will need a habitual vice grip to change it.

How do our children see their own future? We wonder what dreams have formed and developed over their more impressionable years. A literal and reality-based goal-setting approach is a good tool to have in practice for any child, and ours are no different. I mean, I wanted to be a rock star. That's practical, right?

Jagger sees his future clearly and extremely optimistically, as we all tend to do at that age. His hopes and dreams outweigh any adversity that could take control of certain situations. His goal is fairly practical, though: He wants to be a programmer for Nintendo. At the tender age of 11, we have been able to impress upon him the importance of finding something you love to do and working hard to learn it and make it your source of income. So, as a practical measure, we work toward guiding his skill sets within all facets of the programming world. We expose him to the many types of programming and what those skills can offer him and future employers.

The dynamic between an employer and employee is also going to be a difficult thing to master. As parents we traverse complicated and sometimes stressful jobs and can foresee that it may be hard for him to adjust to certain environments. We talk things through with him. He often provides impressive direct and honest insight. We try to teach him about life by sharing our own struggles. Of course, we only talk about appropriate things, but it's important that he understand that life can be difficult and you have to problem solve your way through it.

Long-term focus also is an issue. Unless it's a video game, an hour of anything is asking a lot of Jagger's patience and attention. He usually can hang willingly and positively during that hour but can fade if a task runs longer than anticipated. This is the slow race in the game, and with parental patience, it will be overcome. Consistency is key. We are now working on spending longer durations within multiple-step tasks. It's a daily process, but one that is paying off.

Jagger clearly sees a path to moving out of our house. However, he also alludes to liking the comforts of living at home. We may just find a house magically spring up in our backyard, which would be fine with me. But in an effort to prep him for the real world, he has chores: He helps with shopping; he makes grocery lists; we talk about bills; and we instill a realistic picture of what having a family means. He fondly speaks of finding a suitable girlfriend and getting married. He sees himself as being a good father and role model to his future children. The thought of him fathering children is such an overwhelming and beautiful vision. That innocence we all find attractive has found a way to thrive and continue as he grows.

The subject of love within a marriage or romantic relationship is a struggle for every parent, regardless of whether your child is on the spectrum. Just because children with ASD might process differently doesn't mean they should be treated any differently in terms of appropriate knowledge and education. Jagger asks a lot of questions about sex, and we give honest answers. It's hard not to worry, but we do our best to equip him with love, respect, and honesty. We actually watch a lot of sitcoms and talk through the different situations. We point out the positive and negative behaviors. This has been a really effective tool for us in teaching him the dynamics of relationships.

Overall, we maintain high expectations, expose him to life by putting him in uncomfortable situations, and let him figure things out. When given room to stretch and grow, he does. He amazes us. He figures things out. He can problem-solve. The world will not adapt to him; he has to have the tools to navigate this world, and the only way to do that is by exposing him to life. We will always be there to guide him, but this is his life and we intend for him to choose his own path. Our job is to make sure we have given him the tools to do so. Right now we are always there to catch him, but one day that may not be the case. We want to make sure he is equipped to figure out and navigate a complicated and wonderful world.

When we look over the 8 years since his diagnosis, it's amazing how much Jagger has grown and how far he has come along the path. He works hard. He's aware of his differences, and he has the desire to learn and master social graces. Lastly, he has learned to embrace his diagnosis. He is proud of who he is, because he is awesome. He sees a way of life beyond what we as parents may see, and it couldn't be more inspirational and beautiful.

What Will He Do With His Life?

Before I even met Oscar for the first time, I got to know him through the stories of his day-to-day adventures. I found him to be fascinating. In many ways, he was the star of my favorite reality TV show.

Oscar was 7 years old and in the first grade when he came into my life. His mom was Christina, my high school sweetheart with whom I recently had rekindled a romantic relationship after 17 years. At the time, I was living in Pennsylvania and Christina in Illinois. We certainly put the *long* in long-distance relationship—700-plus miles door to door—and thus would spend countless hours each day sharing the details of our lives through phone conversations.

Christina had two sons, Oscar and 3-year-old Dominic, and would talk about them, as you would expect any mother would. Dominic was like a wind-up toy with new batteries, nonstop and full of life. He was a sucker for fish and chicken noodle soup, loved Angry Birds, and both worshipped and fought with his older brother.

And what about Oscar? Well, the stories about him were definitely ... different.

Though as a rule a quiet and docile child, he also could be counted on for the most ill-timed emotional outbursts. For example, there was the one night he missed out on dessert. Sure, who wouldn't be bummed out not to get that brownie you were looking forward to? Oscar, however, responded like there was a death in the family. "The brownies are gone! Whyyyyyyy?" he wailed from behind the living room couch, where he could be found curled up in the fetal position.

Oftentimes, Christina would talk about Oscar and say, "My child is a vampire." In many ways, she was right. He was overly sensitive to bright lights and loud noises. He would recoil—at times, thrashing violently—to any foreign touch, such as having his bare feet on the grass in his backyard or even getting a hug from his mother.

For Oscar, going to bed never was a simple task because it required he be joined by a specific group of sleeping partners. From toys to books, even a bag of his favorite cinnamon raisin bread, everything had a place. Their spot in the bed took priority, even if it meant he had to contort his body into the remaining space in the most uncomfortable sleeping position. His favorite possession was a worn, disheveled towel that he would promptly place in his mouth. No towel meant zero sleep for everyone in the house.

I would regularly hear about homework, how his mother would walk him through his assignments, only to hit the same brick wall each night. Once there, Oscar would simply stop. That's when 4+4 became 2 and the default answer to most every question would become, "I don't know." Any attempts to push through would result in a crying child and a grouchy parent.

All of this was Oscar. Every day there was a new story, and I couldn't wait to hear each one. They made me laugh. They baffled me. They left me angry—with him and what I thought he was putting his mother through. At the time, there was no explanation for his behaviors. As I saw it, it was his fault. I had a daughter from a previous marriage, and that, of course, made me an expert on parenting and child development. From my perspective, all Oscar needed was a consistent male presence in his life and a new approach to structure and discipline. Introduce that and it would mean a brand-new child.

I proved myself to be horribly naive about everything.

As I write this, 4 years have passed. Oscar is now 11 and in fifth grade. He no longer is a long-distance stranger to me. He is my son (with no "step" label attached). Christina and I have been married for almost three years. As it tends to do, time has brought with it a new perspective and understanding.

The explanation for Oscar's behaviors that had been missing in the beginning finally was provided during his year in the third grade. Despite the struggles at home, Christina could find solace in the Oscar she heard about from his schoolteachers, a "great kid" whose grade card showed no warning signs of any issues. Although she would often ask me, "What am I doing wrong?" at least the problem was isolated. The goal was to figure out what was happening at home.

That changed starting in the third grade. His grades plummeted. "Homework Oscar," the child whose brain nightly reached an impenetrable stopping point, revealed himself in the classroom. The emotional outbursts that were commonplace at home showed up in school, and the "great kid" soon found himself in detention. Oscar drew the attention of the right people—people who asked questions and wanted to find out what was happening. The answer? Oscar was diagnosed as being on the autism spectrum.

It might strike some people as odd that I considered this to be fantastic news. In many ways, it was a relief to hear, because so many things suddenly made complete sense. It wasn't a solution to any problem, that's for sure. But now the obstacles were clear. I wasn't a terrible parent (my tough love approach had already proven to be a flop). My wife wasn't doing anything wrong. We needed a different approach, a different path to helping our child.

Now, as I continue to get to know Oscar, I find myself not angry when I see behaviors I know he struggles to control. Instead, I find myself worried. Worried for him. Worried for his future. Worried for his mother and me. When this story is updated in 10 years, 20 years, how will it read?

Although Oscar's obstacles in life have become clear, it doesn't mean the day-to-day struggles have vanished. I'm fond of telling others that raising children is akin to training future adults. Each day, I catch a glimpse of Oscar, the future adult. It's not always pretty. I'm left asking if it's possible for him to survive alone in the outside world.

Take his grades, for instance, which continue to be a roller coaster. Now his mother and I have a better understanding of how he learns. His mother, in particular, has become a master at relaying information to Oscar in precisely a way that he can digest it, understand it, and give it back to her. That requires time and patience. For Oscar, it has meant taking a gigantic step back in several subjects and receiving instruction outside the normal classroom setting. Even with this attention, he still struggles when asking for help. If he doesn't understand instructions or expectations, he simply stops working.

My wife and I both have graduate degrees in our chosen fields and understand, without question, the value of an education. We also know the financial and social struggles those in our families have faced when they've tackled the outside world without a college degree. Is college possible for my son? It seems like a giant mountain for him to climb.

What will he do with his life? Oscar is a video game fanatic. The goal is simple. Beat the level. Win the game, or lose the game. He values that reliable structure and if given rules will follow them. Those rules must be precise, even written out, and the person giving those rules will need to explain them constantly. Mundane tasks such as closing the garage door, remembering to turn off a light or go to bed, must be reinforced on a daily basis. What happens when the tasks have greater consequences? Is there a job out there that will provide Oscar with a daily road map, a step-by-step, hour-by-hour guide of what to accomplish and how to accomplish it?

Could he emotionally handle life outside the protected environment of a home or school? He has learned to better express his own feelings of frustration and anger. As a result, the once regular emotional outbursts have diminished in quantity. But that doesn't mean they still don't surface.

His biggest hurdle now is to understand that other people have their own feelings that need to be recognized and respected. Detention at school wasn't a one-time isolated incident. He's been a return visitor, once for hitting a classmate who disagreed with his favorite Teenage Mutant Ninja Turtle. In this instance, he also failed to recognize that he actually was the one in trouble. Instead, he celebrated the extra homework time that detention provided him.

In the grand scheme of things, it seems like a trivial incident now. But what will happen in the future when he says the wrong thing to the wrong person at the wrong time? It's a certainty that not everyone will be as understanding to him as his teachers, classmates, and parents.

Is there a world out there in which my son can live in by himself? My wife and I each will turn 50 the year our younger son, Dominic, graduates high school. I'm not afraid to say that we've happily discussed the idea of the so-called empty nest and the opportunities it would provide to us to travel, spend time as a couple, and even pursue different career opportunities. Each time, the conversation usually includes the line, "If Oscar ever moves out of the house."

I try to remind myself to be patient and not to look too far ahead. Oscar has taken giant leaps in the 4 years I've known him. With time and attention, he will continue to take steps toward managing, understanding, and conquering the world he lives in. Then I think of the boy who once had to be reminded that getting dressed was a key first step toward catching the school bus … and I laugh … and I shake my head … and I wonder, "What's going to happen?"

Summary

There's a fine line between being a "helicopter parent" and recognizing your child needs some additional support to thrive in this world. Parenting on the spectrum requires you to have multiple irons in the fire, necessitating repeated conversations and skill development in self-advocacy and education, as well as in the worlds of work, housing, and relationships. These moving targets will keep you busy for years. Just as one developmental stage is mastered, your child moves on to the next challenging one.

Books available to support this topic include the following:

- *Asperger Syndrome and Adolescence: Helping Pre-teens and Teens Get Ready for the Real World,* by Theresa Bolick, PhD
- *Getting a Life With Asperger's: Lessons Learned on the Bumpy Road to Adulthood,* by Jesse A. Saperstein
- *Raising Resilient Children With Autism Spectrum Disorders: Strategies for Helping Them Maximize Their Strengths, Cope With Adversity, and Develop a Social Mindset,* by Robert Brooks, PhD, and Sam Goldstein
- *Raising Martians: From Crash-Landing to Leaving Home: How to Help a Child With Asperger Syndrome or High-Functioning Autism,* by Joshua Muggleton

Closing Thoughts

We would like to extend a sincere thank you to the parents and step-parents who submitted narratives for this book. We had the delight of working with families from across the nation, across time zones, and with varied approaches to writing. Our parents were eager to share their experiences with others—moments of vulnerability as well as moments of triumph. Parents chose to share their insights to be the voice that they wanted or needed along the way and to share their wisdom with the next group of parents starting the journey.

The approach to writing was as varied as the experiences described. Our contributors wrote while wrapping up college semesters and planning weddings, tending to their elderly and at times ill parents, planning funerals, preparing for new babies, and moving across the country. Our contributors wrote in their heads while doing dishes, and scribbled on scraps of paper while waiting for soccer practice to end. We received phone calls with ideas, e-mails with first paragraphs, and half drafts looking for feedback. We also received a bunch of "I got this!" e-mails when we, quite frankly, weren't sure *we* had this! And then, just like parenting, we found our rhythm.

Writing and parenting—kinda the same. Both are done while doing dishes, while waiting for babies to be born, and while taking care of others. Both have moments of "I am completely lost, but I want to nail this!" and "I got this!" Both involve feedback, a desire to nurture others, and some bewilderment.

Given the rates of diagnosis for autism spectrum disorder, you are likely surrounded by people who understand your child. Some of these individuals you already know: teachers, therapists, and other parents. And then there are the invisible others: the cashier at the grocery store, a neighbor down the street, or the teller at the bank. (Seriously, I did meet at teller at a bank who has a child with autism!)

In the spirit of this book, we encourage you to reach out. Give and receive feedback and support, be an advocate, be a soft place to land. Sometimes you will laugh and celebrate the amazing child you are raising, and sometimes you will bring the wine and tissues. Parenting is hard. Parenting on the autism spectrum is harder still. But clearly, you are not alone.

Glossary

applied behavioral analysis (ABA): An innovative treatment backed by research and designed to promote behavior change in children with autism. Initial programs required 40 hours per week of intervention and were quite successful in helping children develop new skills. ABA is a reward-based program with a great deal of data collection and is often provided in both the public school system and the private sector.

Asperger's, Aspie, Aspergirl, Aspiemom, Asperhero: While we currently diagnose autism spectrum disorder (ASD), not so long ago there was a diagnosis called Asperger's syndrome. Asperger's was differentiated from autism by subtle differences in language development and the presence of "special interests." Asperger's was seen to be "higher functioning" than a diagnosis of autism. When the American Psychiatric Association revised the *Diagnostic and Statistical Manual of Mental Disorders* (*DSM*) in 2013, we lost Asperger's and now have ASD. When we had Asperger's available as a diagnosis, a variety of friendly slang was invented: Aspie, Aspergirl, etc. These were all intended to be friendly terms, generally used by "insiders" (i.e., you need to be part of the special ASD club to use the words; if you have a family member, or you provide lots of services to this client group, you're in!). Of note, Asperger's still is a valid diagnosis in other countries, just not, exactly, in the United States. Also, the World Health Organization's *International Classification of Diseases* (10th revision; *ICD-10*) codes are used for American billing purposes, and they actually differentiate between Autism and Asperger's—so who is confused now??

developmental screening or developmental questionnaire: These paper-and-pencil measures are completed by parents at well-child visits (your regular pediatrician visits) and are a great way to quickly assess whether a child is gaining skill in a timely manner. Developmental screenings often look at motor development (Is your child sitting/ crawling/walking?) by certain ages; social emotional development (Does your child respond to his or her name? Does your child bring your things to share in the fun?); and verbal development: Is your child talking in the way we predict for that age range (a certain number of words, complexity of sentences, and use of language for social communication, not just getting needs met)? Most children "pass" the questionnaires, and parents never understand the pivotal role the questionnaires can take in a well-child visit. Children with autism often show such red flags as language delays that prompt referrals for additional evaluations.

Diagnostic and Statistical Manual of Mental Disorders **(DSM):** The American Psychiatric Association's *Diagnostic and Statistical Manual of Mental Disorders* provides the standard criteria for classifying mental disorders, including autism spectrum disorders (ASDs). The fifth edition (*DSM-5*) has been in use since 2013. Substantial changes were made to the classification of ASDs from the previous edition (the *DSM-IV*).

individualized education program (IEP): Some children in the public school system qualify for additional supports and interventions, such as speech-language therapy or extended time for exams. Children who qualify are offered special education services, and the IEP is the document crafted by a team (including parents) to meet the needs of the student.

living on the spectrum: Language holds meaning, and if you are part of select groups, you even get to use special slang terms. Back in the day, we used the word *autistic* (as in "Aidan is autistic"), then we thought about people first ("Aidan has autism"). Although some now prefer the term *autistic* (like fashion, sometimes phrases make a comeback!), others have gone in another direction, referencing things such as "living on the (autism) spectrum." This term is intended to encompass the notion that autism affects virtually all areas of life, and thus the person is "living on the spectrum." On occasion, you even hear great jokes like, "We were on the spectrum, but now we live two streets over!"

neurotypical (NT): While we once used phrases such as *normal* or *a normal control* (in publications describing academic research) to describe people, we now have upgraded these phrases to *neurotypical* (NT). For example, autism, attention-deficit/hyperactivity disorder, and schizophrenia (and other diagnoses) are understood to have neurobiological underpinnings. As such, we believe neurology or "wiring" has something to do with the diagnosis. People who do not have autism or another neurobiological disorder are described as neurotypical, or NT for short. (To integrate our glossary: NTs do *not* live on the spectrum.)

occupational therapist (OT): An occupational therapist helps individuals with illness, injury, or, in this case, developmental delays, achieve the skills they need to live successfully. Sometimes interventions will address sensory needs, and sometimes interventions will address organizational concerns, self-regulation, and promoting independence.

psychologist, psychiatrist, and other mental health professionals: If you are reading this book, you probably have a mental health professional in your life. *Psychologists* have a PhD or a PsyD (a graduate degree) in psychology; you can call these folks "Doctor," and they can help with everything from diagnostics to everyday problem solving. *Psychiatrists* are medical doctors (MDs), and you can call them "Doctor," too. Psychiatrists don't get to do much talk therapy or behavioral therapy these days, but they are mighty helpful with medications. Wait lists for psychiatrists can be long, and it often makes sense to interview psychiatrists long before you are ready to commit to medication. The term *mental health professionals* includes social workers, master's level therapists, counselors, school counselors, and more. There are no doctors in this category. If you have stress in your life (and if you are alive, you probably do), you might want the services of a mental health professional. Be sure to ask about the professional's training in autism spectrum disorder, and find someone who understands you. The research says that the best predictor of success in mental health treatment is the *fit* between therapist and client. Does your provider understand you? Can you two see the world in the same way? If you can, you will likely reach your treatment goals. If you have very different worldviews or you don't feel understood, keep looking until you find the therapist for you. As your developmental needs change, you may need to change therapists. A good therapist will provide referrals and help you transition to the new therapist.

sensory processing disorder (SPD), sensory diets, sensory bins: Some people process sensory information in a manner that does not match the general public. For example, some people are extremely sensitive to sound, lights, taste, or smell. Occupational therapists (OTs) often provide treatment to people with SPD, and treatment often involves intentional exposure to a variety of sensory material (different smells or textures). This intentional exposure is sometimes called a *sensory diet,* where one attempts to expose (or limit) access to sensory material in an effort to help the brain differently process the sensory stimuli. For convenience (think public schools or busy OT practices), the sensory diet is organized into actual containers, and these are often referenced as *sensory bins.* If you have a family member with sensory issues, you may have created a sensory bin (that basket in the corner with all the soft toys? Yep—sensory bin!). You may also be provided with assistance in creating a sensory bin or sensory diet for your loved one.

speech language pathologist (SLP) or speech therapist: We use language to communicate our needs and to connect socially and emotionally. SLPs (or therapists) help people improve their speech or language skills. (They can teach you how to make the "th" sound, but they can also teach you that language is for expressing feelings verbally and how to look toward someone's eyes to read his or her verbal messages.) Outstanding SLPs (thank you, Mallory!) teach people how to get their needs met, accurately read messages from others, and generally how to survive and thrive in life.

stim, stimming, self-stimulatory behaviors: Often, folks with a diagnosis of autism spectrum disorder use motor movements to soothe themselves. These behaviors are often referred to as *stimming* and may look like humming, rocking, flapping the hands, flicking fingers, for example. Although the behaviors are soothing to the person, they can sometimes call attention to the person and create distraction or an uncomfortable social moment for the person or the group of people.

Appendix

Books

Attwood, T. (2008). *The complete guide to Asperger's syndrome*. Philadelphia, PA: Jessica Kingsley.

Bolick, T. (2004). *Asperger syndrome and adolescence: Helping pre-teens and teens get ready for the real world*. Beverly, MA: Fair Winds Press.

Brooks, R., & Goldstein, S. (2012). *Raising resilient children with autism spectrum disorders: Strategies for helping them maximize their strengths, cope with adversity, and develop a social mindset*. New York, NY: McGraw-Hill Education.

Centers for Disease Control and Prevention. (2016). Facts about ASD. Retrieved from www.cdc.gov/ncbddd/autism/facts.html

Chödrön, P. (2000). *When things fall apart: Heart advice for difficult times*. Boulder, CO: Shambhala.

Clark, J. (2010). *Asperger's in pink: Pearls of wisdom from inside the bubble of raising a child with Asperger's*. Arlington, TX: Future Horizons.

Elder, J. (2005). *Different like me: My book of autism heroes*. Philadelphia, PA: Jessica Kingsley.

Fields-Meyer, T. (2011). *Following Ezra: What one father learned about Gumby, otters, autism, and love from his extraordinary son*. New York, NY: New American Library.

Finch, D. (2012). *The journal of best practices: A memoir of marriage, Asperger's syndrome, and one man's quest to be a better husband*. New York, NY: Scribner.

Hall, K. (2000). *Asperger syndrome, the universe and everything*. Philadelphia, PA: Jessica Kingsley.

Jackson, L. (2002). *Freaks, geeks and Asperger syndrome: A user's guide to adolescence*. Philadelphia, PA: Jessica Kingsley.

Muggleton, J. (2011). *Raising Martians—from crash-landing to leaving home: How to help a child with Asperger syndrome or high-functioning autism.* Philadelphia, PA: Jessica Kingsley.

Naseef, R. A. (2012). *Autism in the family: Caring and coping together.* Baltimore, MD: Brookes.

Palmer, A, (2012). *A friend's and relative's guide to supporting the family with autism: How can I help?* Philadelphia, PA: Jessica Kingsley.

Saperstein, J. A. (2016). *Getting a life with Asperger's: Lessons learned on the bumpy road to adulthood.* New York, NY: TarcherPerigee.

Sheahan, B., & DeOrnellas, K. (2011). *What I wish I'd known about raising a child with autism: A mom and a psychologist offer heartfelt guidance for the first five years.* Arlington, TX: Future Horizons.

Verdick, E., & Reeve, E. (2015). *The survival guide for kids with autism spectrum disorders (and their parents).* Golden Valley, MN: Free Spirit.

Welton, J. (2003). *Can I tell you about Asperger syndrome?: A guide for friends and family.* Philadelphia, PA: Jessica Kingsley.

Wine, A. (2005). *What it is to be me!: An Asperger kid book.* Fairdale, KY: Fairdale.

Winner, M. G., & Crooke, P. (2011). *Socially curious, curiously social: A social thinking guidebook for bright teens and young adults.* Great Barrington, MA: North River Press.

Helpful websites

Crawford, L. K. (n.d.). *Holland, Schmolland.* Retrieved from http://www.autism-pdd.net/testdump/test16481.htm

Centers for Disease Control and Prevention. (2016). Facts about ASD. Retrieved from www.cdc.gov/ncbddd/autism/facts.html

Crawford, L.K. (n.d.). Holland, Schmolland. Retrieved from http://www.autism-pdd.net/testdump/test16481.htm

Kingsley, E. P. (1987). *Welcome to Holland.* Retrieved from http://www.our-kids.org/archives/Holland.html

The Melmed Center (Dr. Raun Melmed). Retrieved from melmed-center.com ("The Melmed Center provides a compassionate, state-of-the-art approach to the assessment and treatment of behavioral, educational and developmental challenges in children and adults.")

socialthinking.com: This website was created by speech language pathologists with the goal of improving social communication and social skills across the life span and across settings (home, school, work, community).

Temple Grandin, PhD. Retrieved from templegrandin.com (Dr. Grandin is an American professor of animal science at Colorado State University, world-renowned autism spokesperson, and consultant to the livestock industry on animal behavior. She is known as one of the first individuals on the autism spectrum to publicly share insights from her personal experience of autism.)

wrongplanet.net: This is a forum to post questions and answers about ASD-related topics, including IEPs, dating, working, and resources.

About the Authors

Rachel Bédard, PhD, is a licensed psychologist living and working in Fort Collins, Colorado. Known for her quick wit and dry humor, Dr. Bédard can seemingly find strengths in any situation and guide her fantastic clients to their own version of success. She thanks the many individuals who have allowed her to learn from their life experiences. This book would not have been possible without the inspiration of clients and mentors.

Mallory Griffith, MA, CCC-SLP, is a speech-language therapist who focuses on coaching social communication skills in her private practice. She is the founder of the nonprofit, SOCIAL! The Pendley Project, which supports individuals with social and sensory-based needs through meaningful, daily activities. Mallory is profoundly grateful for clients who provide inspiration and colleagues who kindly support her endeavors. She is particularly thankful for Dr. Bédard's patient mentorship and friendship. Mallory resides and works in Fort Collins, Colorado.

Made in the USA
San Bernardino, CA
21 January 2019